A Beard in Nepal 2

Fiona Roberts

BOOKS

Winchester, UK
Washington, USA

First published by O-Books, 2012
O-Books is an imprint of John Hunt Publishing Ltd., Laurel House, Station Approach,
Alresford, Hants, SO24 9JH, UK
office1@jhpbooks.net
www.johnhuntpublishing.com

For distributor details and how to order please visit the 'Ordering' section on our website.

ISBN: 978 1 84694 444 4

A CIP catalogue record for this book is available from the British Library.

Design: Stuart Davies

Printed and bound by CPI Group (UK) Ltd, Croydon, CR0 4YY

We operate a distinctive and ethical publishing philosophy in all
areas of our business, from our global network of authors to
production and worldwide distribution.

Contents

Keep up to date with books by Fiona Roberts at:
www.spanglefish.com/fionaroberts

ALSO BY FIONA ROBERTS:
A BEARD IN NEPAL
Our First Trip to the Village

GHOST OF A SMILE
Memories from a Medium's Life

Dedication

This book is dedicated to Tod, my wonderful, long-suffering better half, without whom my life would be very dull indeed!

Chapter One

At the time of writing this book Nepal is jostling for the inauspicious position of twelfth on the list of the world's poorest countries.

Having been there or thereabouts for many years on the scale of the haves and the have nots, Nepal's present position doesn't look like changing anytime soon – not for the better, at least.

Tod and I are not so blinkered and unaware of humanity's myriad problems that we knew nothing of the plight of the impoverished, as they struggle to simply exist in so many parts of the globe today. But it was not until we actually *went* to Nepal and spent time there that the on the ground reality of being so poor as a nation really struck home with us.

That which *we* take for granted everyday, never giving it a second thought, often simply just does not exist in Nepal and if it *does*, it can seem something of a sad parody.

For example, there *is* electricity in the capital city of Kathmandu, but only for a maximum of eight hours in every twenty-four, and then often late at night. Imagine trying to run a business under those conditions.

There *is* a public water supply system in Kathmandu, but this is usually only turned on once a week for a short time. Unless you have a water-storage tank you are at the mercy of the stand-pipes, and will have to fill your containers with the often filthy water which needs to be boiled before it is safe to drink. And did I mention that in many areas the standpipes are turned on at 2am? Unsurprisingly, I suppose, an increasing number of the population are being struck down by waterborne diseases.

The pursuit of money takes on added significance in a country where there is so little of it, and of course human nature running sadly true to form, corruption and dishonesty will follow as a result, closing their callous, grasping fists around whatever they can reach.

I mention this because on our second trip to Nepal Tod and I became very much aware of, and indeed involved in some of the sadder consequences of the darker side of human nature.

In 2009 we spent five months in Nepal, most of that time living in the small, isolated village of Salle (pronounced Solley) high up in the Himalayas, not far from Everest Base Camp. We went there to teach English.

We also spent time in Kathmandu, braving the somewhat, nay *definitely*, perilous journey back to the capital, occasionally scrambling over landslides along the way, and frequently being thrown around in micro buses for ten or more hours at a time, whilst being deafened by the world's loudest music. Oh joy!

We were lucky enough to visit Tibet too, and I shall be eternally grateful to that incredible country for providing me with the opportunity to shout gleefully, and at the top of my voice, "Yippee! Yaks!" as I stood at the edge of a vast, silent swathe of flat valley floor which stretched far away into the misty distance, and through which a crystal-clear river meandered peacefully.

Not a single yak paid me the slightest attention. They just munched and meditated, at one with that astonishing landscape at the top of the world.

Peaceful creatures, yaks.

We were completely smitten with the inhabitants of Salle – adults, children and animals alike – and our return trip to Nepal was designed specifically to see them all again. We wanted to take presents to them.

The village of Salle is situated along one steep side of a valley in the Everest region of Nepal, about 200km north east of Kathmandu.

The village itself remains today much as it has been for many hundreds of years, and the villagers carry on their lives in much the same way as their grandparents did, and as *their* grand-parents did before *them*.

They grow crops on the flat terraces that they have cut out of the steep valley sides – potatoes, maize and corn. They eat the potatoes, feed the corn to the chickens, and use the maize to make raxi, the local lip-burning firewater.

We also saw some very strange-looking squash plants growing wild. They grew as big as triffids in a frighteningly short space of time, and although the villagers didn't actually cultivate them they did pick and eat the squash.

(For a *much* fuller description of village life please see our first book!)

Few 'outsiders', and even fewer white people have ever set foot in Salle.

For sure that has a lot to do with its remoteness and inaccessibility, and I must admit there were times when I thought *I* was not going to be able to set foot in Salle, as I puffed and wheezed, gasped and sweated, slid and tripped all the way up the mountain and down into the valley.

If I'm honest I think I may *never* have reached the village on several occasions had it not been for the gallant efforts of Tod and Kalyani. Their combined pushing, pulling, and nifty grabbing of my flailing arms and other parts of my anatomy kept me attached, albeit perilously, to the side of the mountain, and prevented me from plummeting down to the valley floor considerably faster, and with much greater ease than I had come up.

During all their hard work I never heard a single word of reproach from either of them, although I did catch a couple of exchanged glances featuring eyes rolled upwards. I pretended not to notice. I knew where my interests lay.

Kalyani was the young headmistress of the Junior school where we taught English. It is about an hour's trek away from the village through the still, silent forest that breathes down your neck, muffles your footsteps, and makes you want to whisper.

There surely has never been a more spectacular setting for a school. I say school and most of us think of rather dingy brick-built constructions, but *this* school consists of two large, one-story wooden huts, divided into five classrooms, inside which you will find bare wooden tables and rough wooden benches. Not a mod con in sight, only a blackboard and chalk. There is no electricity, no water, and no toilet.

The huts stand on the sun baked clay of a massive, flat clearing high up in the forest, and the view from that point never ceased to take our breath away.

Across the valley, seeming almost close enough to touch, their steep sides clothed in green forest, and their peaks thickly capped with gleaming, glinting snow, stood a mighty range of mountains. On just two occasions we were privileged to see the habitual thick wall of cloud behind these mountains disperse, revealing the awesome Everest range.

The children come from miles around to attend the school, and to reach it a trek of anywhere between thirty and sixty minutes through the forest and up the mountain is considered normal. They love their school, not because it is situated in one of the world's most beautiful spots, but because it provides them with an education. Even at their young ages they know that they are lucky. Truancy is non-existent – how cool is that? Late attendance may sometimes happen because it took longer than expected to feed the animals, cut the wood, or fetch the water.

Kalyani, at twenty, is the youngest headmistress I've ever met. She looked after us during our stay in Nepal – nothing was too much trouble for her where we were concerned. Amongst other things, she hated to see us carrying anything and would simply grab whatever it was – maybe a rucksack or a pile of exercise books – and trot off with it up or down a mountain, ignoring our protestations. She became known as our 'Pack Ant', this being a reference to the fact that she was small (barely five-feet tall) but very strong and active. She is actually something akin to a small human dynamo.

Kalyani has a wicked sense of humour. Add to that the fact that she found us very strange and very funny and you'll understand that the three of us spent a great deal of time laughing together. Her English is pretty good and she acted as our translator, particularly in the village where there was usually no one else around who spoke English.

After we left Nepal in August 2009 to return to the UK, we tried to stay in contact with Kalyani and the villagers. Easier said than done. The first few letters we sent did not reach the village. Kalyani told us they had most probably been stolen, opened in the hope that as they were from abroad they might contain money.

And in fact, during one of our many journeys in Nepal we shared a micro bus with, among others, a postman. To our absolute horror we saw that he was opening some of the envelopes entrusted to his care, looking through their contents, extracting whatever he fancied, and then throwing what remained out of the bus window.

Kalyani does have a mobile phone but making contact with it high up in the Himalayas, where the signal can easily be distorted, was no easy matter. But we managed it, and have enjoyed many happy conversations consisting of, "Hello, hello" and, "Bye bye, bye bye" as Kalyani passed her phone round the listening villagers and children.

It was of course a forgone conclusion that we would return to Salle one day.

During our stay, whenever we had left the village to return to Kathmandu or go travelling somewhere, the children had always asked us to bring them a present back.

"What would you like?" Tod asked them on the eve of our first departure. Mistake! He was immediately engulfed in screaming, laughing children, climbing up onto him and pulling his beard. The beard pulling bit was habitual, everyone did it, the adults too. Tod didn't mind. Just as well really, because they were absolutely fascinated by his long, bushy beard, and it went before us everywhere, rather like a large fluffy beacon.

Ask your average European or American ten-year-old what present he or she would like. The answer is going to be something computerish, or fashionable clothing, maybe trainers, isn't it?

You may not be surprised to learn that the children of Salle all wanted shampoo, toothpaste, socks, games, pencils and English books.

The reason is obvious. They do not have these items, and have no way of obtaining most of them.

We discovered that the shops catering for tourists in Kathmandu sold just about everything you might need, but at a very high price. We took what we could back to the village, and the magical appearance of half a dozen bottles of hair shampoo from out of Tod's rucksack led to 'The Great Hair Wash Day'.

Early in 2011 we told Kalyani that we were coming back to the village and asked her what we could bring for the children and adults.

"Oh!" she squealed, "Just yourselves! We want to see you and you don't have to bring anything with you!"

But of course we wanted to, and pretty soon friends and colleagues and their children were giving us books, pens, soap and any number of other things to take with us.

Please don't get the idea that the villagers of Salle are living in poverty – far from it. They certainly don't consider themselves to be poor, and will always point out that they have everything they need for their lives in the village.

To some extent, of course, poverty is relative; however, a difficult grey area has crept into the equation over the past few years where the village of Salle is concerned. The children in particular, and now many of the adults too, have some idea, however vague, of how we in the West live, and of what we take for granted in our lives...

We told Kalyani that we didn't want to inadvertently cause insult, or any kind of problem by bringing presents that were unacceptable up to the village.

Could we bring make-up for the girls? What about sweets? Was it ok to give the children thermal vests? And what about socks for the men? Would the women wear thermal vests too?

Kalyani laughed kindly at our questions, and our rucksacks began to fill up and up...and up.

Chapter Two

Our second trip to Nepal started in much the same way as the first - I whinged until Tod picked my rucksack up and carried it to the car.

It was heavy. Even *he* had to agree.

Both rucksacks were filled to the absolute limit – 23kg – and our hand luggage was up to the permitted maximum of 7kg. Plus I was carrying, or trying to, a very very big handbag and *that* was full too.

But *this* time we had with us just *one* change of clothing each; our life-saving water-filter bottles; a small torch; a pair of toothbrushes; and my magnifying mirror – Tod had sneakily tried to leave that out, but I'd sneakily put it back in. Fellow human bats will probably appreciate my need for said object.

We had even, although only after much animated discussion, decided not to take our sleeping bags – our lovely warm, thick, soft and comfortable sleeping bags with hoods – the very ones which had protected us from those large, black, hairy, *poisonous spiders* which had run riot in our room in the village.

Let me explain:

Just before we left the UK for Nepal in 2009 I went out for dinner one evening with a group of close friends. It was a 'farewell and good luck for the trip' dinner.

I could tell by the identical expressions of mild to moderate astonishment that they all wore as they stared at me that my friends thought I was a loony.

I had just admitted to being a *bit* nervous about what the next five months might hold in store for Tod and me when Maria, ever tactful bless her, asked if I'd seen a particular TV programme the previous week. I hadn't.

"Oh pity, then you missed the bit about the spiders in Nepal," she said, and I swear she chuckled.

Now spiders are my one big fear, and I'd go as far as to say that there's quite obviously something in the human psyche that has 'Fear of Spiders' deeply engraved on it in copperplate gothic, bold, size twenty. I cannot even *say* the word 'spider' without feeling eight hairy legs descending my spine.

"Apparently there's a really poisonous spider in Nepal that has eight eyes," Maria continued gleefully, seemingly oblivious to the fact that I'd stopped chewing my garlic bread with cheese, and was staring at her.

"Don't you mean eight *legs*?" Carmel asked her. Sensible girl, Carmel.

"No," Maria said, "*Eyes!* Eight *eyes*! You should have seen them! The eyes sort of stand up and swivel! All of them! They can see behind!"

I groaned.

"*And* they're poisonous," she added with a bit of a shiver in my direction, in case I hadn't noted that fact the *first* time she'd said it.

Without a doubt I'd rather not have been privy to this information at *any* time, but especially not just before entering the spider's den, so to speak. Lovely girl Maria, but I'd p'raps be making a small adjustment to my Christmas-card list later in the year.

A couple of weeks after that well remembered dinner Tod and I had just arrived half a world away, seven thousand feet up in the village of Salle, and were recovering from the rigours of the journey there.

I don't wish to bore you by repeating verbatim those descriptions which you may already have read in our first book but...

Our room was upstairs in a village house. It was reached by an external wooden staircase which passed through a wooden trapdoor and emerged onto a wooden veranda at the top of the house. The houses are all made of...local stone.

We spent most of our first day in the village sitting on this veranda, just staring across the deep wide valley that lay in front of us at the jigsaw rows of terraces running down the opposite side. Away to our right at the end of the valley we could see the beginning of the Everest range.

The air was clear, the sky was startlingly blue. The calming sounds of everyday life in an isolated Himalayan valley floated up to us – a water buffalo calling (nice voices, water buffalo); an eagle screeching far overhead, its massive wings resting on the thermal currents; and the sound of leafy branches being chopped from a tree for the goats' lunch – all intermingled with the laughter of children at play...

Those leafy branches, the goats' lunch branches, are chopped down by the *older* village women. They have to climb towards the top of the tree to reach the smaller branches, and the trees can be thirty- or forty-feet high, often growing perilously close to the edge of the terrace. It is shockingly like watching your Granny clambering up a tree with a long-bladed knife clutched between her teeth.

We had two beds in our room. I use the word 'bed' loosely because I don't think anything lacking a mattress can really be called a bed. We piled the schoolbooks, posters, pencils and paper that we had brought with us for the school on one bed, and laid our sleeping bags on the other, directly onto the bare wooden slats.

We were so tired the first night that we slept right through, and didn't really notice how uncomfortable the bed was.

But the instant my posterior touched down on those hard wooden slats on our second night there I realised that I was a spoilt Westerner, and wasn't going to be able to sleep. I took a deep breath and did a bit of strategic whinging. It had the desired effect.

By the way, the next time you're planning a few months away in an isolated village high in the Himalayas, you need to take a 'Tod' with you. There is nothing he cannot turn his hand to, nothing he won't tackle, and very few, if any, situations defeat him. He also has a great sense of humour, and a tendency to ignore me and my whinging.

This particular challenge was a no brainer for him.

Having spread our spare clothes over the bed's offending bare wooden base we settled down in our sleeping bags. Tod started snoring almost immediately. It took me a lot longer.

I was already awake when the village began to come to life as dawn broke. I lay unmoving in the dark and listened, trying to identify each unfamiliar noise that floated in through the glassless windows of our room: splashing water somewhere near by; the swift, skilful lighting of an open fire; shoeless feet running past, pounding on the hard baked clay surface; children in the next house sneaking down the creaky outside steps; a couple of water buffalo ambling past mumbling and snorting; chickens scratching for seeds…

The faint light of a warm, new Himalayan day began to slip into the room through the cracks in the wooden window shutters, and objects around me began to emerge from the dense gloom.

I lay on my back looking up at the wooden beams of the low ceiling above me, wondering if I would ever walk normally again. I ached all over. I wondered if there was anything else 'we' could do to make the bed more comfortable. How many nights were there in five months? Would I survive? Could Tod somehow make us a mattress? Huummm.

Little by little the overhead beams became clearer, defined by the strengthening daylight in the room. The darkness of the uneven gaps between them grew even darker as the shadows inched across the room, pushed by the encroaching daylight.

Directly above my head a patch of darkness moved along a beam. By the time my tired, altitude-numbed brain had analysed the image and realised that this was no shadow, the black patch had stopped moving.

"Tod!" I nudged him, never taking my eyes off the patch on the beam.

Silence.

"Tod!" I said louder, "There's something on the ceiling."

"Huumm? What?" he said, his voice muffled from inside the sleeping bag.

"There's something moving on the ceiling, something insecty...Oh my God," I said shakily, "it could be a spider!"

"What time is it?" Tod asked.

"Does that *matter*?" I said somewhat testily, "It's *big*, and it's moving again. Aarrrgh!" and I squirmed across the bed to Tod's side, to get out from underneath whatever it was, in case it was into abseiling.

"How many eyes has it got?" Tod said and, I kid you not, he chuckled. I felt that was entirely inappropriate given the situation.

"You wouldn't be laughing if it fell on you," I said, "It's ten times bigger than an English insect, whatever it is!"

Tod's head emerged from his sleeping bag, and he blinked at me in the half daylight which by now filled the room.

"You haven't got your glasses on, Magoo," he said, grinning, "I'm surprised you could even see the *beam*, let alone something wandering along it!"

He can be so hurtful sometimes.

"Look! It's *there*!" I said pointing, but wouldn't you know it the beam was bare, and there was no sign of any life form on it, or anywhere else that we could see.

Tod went back to sleep.

Getting dressed later was a bit of a nightmare. We picked our clothes up gingerly and shook them at a prudent distance, in case something insecty had snuck in there amongst the folds. In fact, that was something we did every day in Nepal, even in the hotel in Kathmandu. But the stranger on the beam was nowhere to be seen.

I could tell by the way Tod looked at me that he thought I'd imagined it, but he remained tactfully silent.

That day Kalyani took us to see the school for the first time.

Arriving back in the village in the late afternoon after trekking (or in *my* case slipping and falling) up and down mountains and through forests, while struggling with the increasingly debilitating effects of altitude, we were glad to sit down in our room for a rest.

Tod sat on the bed and lent back against the wall, his legs stretched out in front of him.

The villagers have no use for chairs. In their houses they sit on the hard clay floor on thin bamboo mats, so chairs are few and far between in Salle. In actual fact a good chair is about as common in Nepal as a plump whippet. However, they had found one especially for us, and I now sat gratefully down on it, facing Tod.

Something of the calm peacefulness of the village and valley settled on the room, and the long evening shadows began to reach in through the glassless windows.

Tod closed his eyes, and I picked up my book intending to make the most of the dwindling daylight to read a chapter or two.

There was complete silence inside our room, outside on the terrace, and far across the valley. Peace hung in the still, calm air.

Five minutes later I turned a page and glanced in Tod's direction. I froze, and the hairs on the back of my neck scrambled upright. There, moving slowly and steadily up the wall no more than a few inches from Tod's shoulder was a massive black spider.

As I opened my mouth to shout a warning Tod sensed the movement beside him and opened his eyes. Before you could scream, *"Arachnophobia!"* he was off the bed and across the room, where I joined him pdq.

"Bloody Hell!" he said quietly, but with considerable feeling,

"That's big!"

Bit of an understatement actually!

We both stared wide-eyed at the now immobile monster on the wall. It was probably about three inches across its hairy back, not including quite a stocky set of equally hairy legs. It stared back at us.

"Did you happen to notice how many eyes it has?" I whispered.

Tod ignored me.

I'm sorry to say that it was a case of 'the spider or us', and Tod picked up a large, heavy cardboard tube that had contained a number of posters for the school, and did the necessary.

Later that evening we told Kalyani about our unwelcome visitor, and described the spider as best we could. She shook her head and looked perplexed,

"I don't know a spider like that," she told us, "Nothing like that comes into our houses. But I'll come and look in case there are some more."

I really really hoped there would *not* be any more, and in fact, although we all searched carefully in every corner of our room, under the beds and along the ceiling beams, we found nothing that might indicate that we were sharing our room with anything more sinister than flying cockroaches, and *they* were actually quite cute. Measuring about an inch and a half across their shiny green or blue metallic coloured backs, they are the comedians of the flying insect world. Most nights Tod would have to turn at least a couple of them the right way up, after they crash landed on the table, having been attracted there to the light of our candles. Sod's Law meant that they fell onto their rounded backs and rocked around, legs kicking in the air, unable to right themselves. Embarrassing.

Kalyani assured us again that spiders of any kind were rare in the village houses, and repeated her assertion that our visitor had been a one off.

But that night Tod and I zipped ourselves tightly into our sleeping bags, pulling the hoods over our heads until just our noses and eyes remained visible. We lay awake long into the warm night like a couple of Egyptian mummies, staring wide-eyed at the blackness of the ceiling above us. Nothing moved there, at least nothing that we could see.

We were tired in the morning and every movement was an effort. I had started to cough – a sure sign of the effects of altitude.

Tod was looking through the piles of school books on the bed, and sorting them into easy to carry loads. He lifted up the cardboard tube – yesterday's murder weapon – and started to put it into a bag of rubbish on the floor, but suddenly stopped.

I looked over at him. He was standing completely still, staring at the cardboard tube in his hand. Something had caught his eye.

The tube usually had a white plastic cap on each end, but one of the caps was missing, unneeded anyway now that the tube had served its usefulness and was empty. But *was* it empty?

Slowly and carefully Tod tipped the open end of the tube towards himself and stared into it.

"Pass me a book," he said quietly, standing perfectly still and holding the tube immobile in front of him.

I stepped over to the bed and picked up a paperback. I didn't know what he'd found but I had a horrible feeling...

"Be careful," I whispered, as I put the book in Tod's free hand.

Placing the paperback carefully over the open end of the tube, and holding it firmly in place, Tod turned to look at me.

"There's one in here," he said.

"One of those spiders?" I squeaked, "In that tube?"

I have often found that a certain amount of stress in a situation may cause me to ask inconsequential, even *inane* questions. This situation was no exception.

"Pass me the parcel tape," Tod said, "I'll tape the end up."

"What for?" I asked nervously, "What are you going to do

15

with it?"

Tod may be slightly bohemian, but even *he* wouldn't want something like that as a pet...would he? Oh dear.

"I'm going to show Kalyani," he said, "I'm sure she'll be interested."

Not long after, Kalyani and her sister, also a teacher, arrived with hot water for us. Every morning they boiled the water over their open fire and brought it to us. We made tea with it, using tea bags we'd brought with us from the UK. Many a time we crossed our fingers and hoped the water had been boiled for long enough to kill anything harmful to us.

We showed the two young women the cardboard tube, and told them what was in it.

"I will take it outside and open it, and then tell you what kind of spider it is," Kalyani said grinning, picking up the tube and heading for the door. We stood well back as she passed us.

We followed her out onto the veranda, and stood watching as she trotted down the stairs and onto the wide, flat area of hard baked clay at the front of the house. A couple of neighbours came to see what she was doing. Half a dozen curious, giggling children appeared. The elderly couple whose house we were lodging in came out from downstairs and joined the small crowd. They all stood in a circle around Kalyani and the tube, laughing and talking, enjoying this unusual distraction, and quite obviously expecting the strange English couple to have been scared by some small insect of absolutely no note.

The villagers waved up at us, pointed to the tube, and made crawly-type movements with their hands amid much laughter.

Right-oh.

So, when Kalyani pulled the end off the tube and a large, black, hairy spider shot out and landed heavily on the ground at her feet, *we* were the only ones not screaming or running. Actually we were grinning, albeit from a safe distance, as we watched the ungainly rout.

When the kerfuffle had died down Kalyani joined us on the balcony.

Interestingly, most of the younger villagers had never seen a spider like that, but the older ones knew it to be a tree-dweller. As there was a large and beautiful tree overhanging the house at the back, this was thought to be the route our 'visitors' had used to access our room.

"Please, please," Kalyani said to us, "do not touch the spiders."

"I can promise you," I told her, "there is *absolutely* no chance at all of our doing that!" I shivered. Perish the thought!

"Why do you say that?" Tod asked her, "Why do you tell us not to touch them?"

"Because they are poisonous," she said, "and here in the village we do not have any medicine. The nearest hospital is at Jiri." She smiled apologetically at us, and glanced around the veranda nervously.

Tod and I looked at each other. Getting to Jiri (the old Everest Base Camp) would necessitate climbing out of the valley and up the mountain, and then somehow covering the twelve kilometres along the road to Jiri. Certainly not an easy journey, even if you hadn't been bitten by a poisonous spider.

Over the next week or so we took extra special care to check under the beds, along the ceiling beams, and in the corners of our room every day. We covered our boots at night, and put our clothes inside closed bags.

But despite our best efforts the arachnids thumbed their noses at us and stubbornly refused to leave. Half a dozen further incidents, not least the afternoon when one of 'them' *ran over* my foot, left us feeling decidedly jumpy.

Kalyani began to talk about us moving into *her* room.

"It would be safer for you," she said, looking nervously around as she handed us our thermos of hot water for the day, "and I could move in with my mother."

We thought she was probably right, but before we needed to make a decision, guess what – the cavalry arrived!

It was still dark when I woke the next morning. All was quiet, but I was sure something had woken me, some unfamiliar sound which had alerted my senses.

"Did you hear something?" I whispered in Tod's direction.

Silence.

"Tod!" I said more loudly, "Did you hear something?"

"What? No!" he mumbled, "Hear what?"

"I'm not sure...something on the roof I think," I said.

We waited, ears at the ready, hardly breathing. All was quiet. The village was still sleeping.

Suddenly, what did we hear but the unmistakable sound of small rodent feet running across the roof space above our heads! We started to giggle. The tiny feet hurriedly crossed the room, paused, and then ran back the way they had come. Wonderful! The tapping of tiny toe nails!

Over the next few days it sounded as if a whole rodent extended family had moved in above us, and some of them wore small boots. We loved listening to them dashing here and there, morning and evening, and had a lot of fun imagining what they were getting up to.

We didn't know if they were mice or rats, or some other furry Nepalese rodent, but quite honestly, if we had to share our accommodation with anyone, give me a rodent rather than a spider any day!

From the moment our furry cavalry moved in we never saw another spider. Which begs the question...

Did the arachnids move out? Were they pushed out? Or did they become tasty rodent snacks?

We'll probably never know. But *we* became spider free.

Yippee!

Chapter Three

On our second visit to Nepal we flew from Manchester to Abu Dhabi. Tod settled into a window seat on the plane and within minutes he was snoring. How does he do it? He could probably sleep on a clothes line.

Before we even took off I noticed a very disagreeable smell floating around. Drains? Surely not.

By the time we were airborne I realised with horror that the gentleman sitting on my other side was suffering from the worst case of halitosis known in the entire history of mankind. I was sitting by a dragon.

Tod kept dozing off, and I kept nudging him and saying useful things like, "Aaarrrrgggghhhh!" and, "Yuuuccckkk!" and, "Can't breathe!" accompanied by dramatic hand-flapping movements, until he passed me the airline brochure from the seat pocket in front of us, and suggested I stand it on my shoulder, thereby separating my face from the offending air stream.

Success! The brochure and I crossed most of Europe and part of the Middle East in this way, with just an occasional bit of joggling needed to accurately deflect the dragon breath.

"Don't worry," Tod said as we disembarked at Abu Dhabi, "you can have a couple of hours sleep here".

We had to change terminals, but we might have actually changed *country* we walked so far. My huge handbag seemed to get heavier and heavier. Eventually we turned a corner and arrived in a building site.

The place was under construction, and was only barely recognisable as an embryonic airport terminal.

Hoards of weary transiting passengers ebbed and flowed round and over the piles of rubble and mini craters in the half-finished corridors. There was no signage, and it took us ages to find an arrow pointing to Gate Three, through which we hoped eventually to find our flight to Kathmandu.

The few seats in the terminal were already taken, their woeful occupants staring glassy-eyed into mid-air, or slumped in uncomfortable shapes, snoring.

We sat on the dusty floor, leant back against our bulging hand luggage, and tried to sleep.

Two hours later it was time to get moving. But I had fossilised where I sat, and Tod had to pull me upright. I creaked and groaned. He smiled at me.

Have you noticed that as you get older, each time you stretch or reach for something, or bend down to pick something off the floor, you give a little grunt or snort? It's true.

Once you catch yourself gently grunting you realise just how often you do it!

Tod set off like a greyhound out the traps in pursuit of Gate Three. I limped wearily after him, dragging my 7kg backpack and massive handbag behind me.

We were not entirely surprised to find that Gate Three was not where it should have been, and no one seemed to know where it had gone. Oddly enough our flight had also disappeared off the screens. Huummm. Yes, we've **all** been there...

We wandered forlornly around like airport flotsam and jetsam, and I had just about lost the will to live when an attendant waved us in a completely different direction, to a different Gate, and a flight with a different number.

But what do you know, this *was* our flight, and we were finally on the last leg of our second journey to Kathmandu.

I muttered a few choice words about never doing this again, and whinged that I was tired, but Tod took no notice so I gave up. He's the strong and silent type. I'm not.

We arrived in Kathmandu at 4pm local time, queued for our Visas, and then walked out of the airport and into the bright sunshine of a Nepalese spring afternoon.

The hotel, the same one we'd stayed in on our last visit, had told us they'd send a micro bus to meet us, so we began looking around for the driver.

"Mr Tod! Mr Tod!" a voice shouted over the habitual loud hubbub which accompanied the human scrum outside the airport.

I started to laugh, "Look!" I said to Tod, "There's our ride!"

A grinning Nepalese driver was jumping up and down and waving a large sheet of paper in the air above his head. Written on the paper was

'Mr Tod. English man with beard'.

"Good description!" I said, still giggling, "Ali Baba's back!"

The driver greeted us warmly, and we got into the micro bus for the thirty-minute drive to the hotel in the Thamel (tourist) area of Kathmandu.

We sat staring out the bus windows, mesmerised. The traffic was still manic, the air was still full of dust and pollution, and the constant noise was just as jumbled and all pervading as we remembered. Oh, and the eternal question remained the same – how on earth does everything and everyone fit onto the jam-packed roads of Kathmandu?

At the hotel we were greeted like old friends. The staff came over to say hello to us and to pull Tod's beard! They wanted to know if we were going up to the village again, and what our plans were. It was really good to see them all.

Then we walked across the narrow road outside the hotel to see our friend Karma. She works in the travel agency that helped us to visit Tibet in 2009, and we had remained in touch with her.

We had Nepali tea, and heard all her news.

Then we rang Kalyani and told her we'd arrived in Kathmandu.

Since we'd left Nepal in 2009 Kalyani had married her long-time boyfriend Nabin, and she now lives in Kathmandu. However, Nabin is studying in Australia, and we are still not clear about how long he will be staying there. So Kalyani lives with her sister in law in a western suburb of the city, and at the moment is filling her days by studying English and IT.

We arranged to meet her at our hotel the next morning.

Time is an arbitrary concept in Nepal...we know that now. Nothing can be hurried. So we pottered about in the morning, sat in the hotel garden and read the local English-language newspapers, and eventually crossed the road to have tea with Karma again.

When we came out of the agency later we immediately spotted Kalyani standing outside the hotel, at the side of the narrow road, in the shade cast by the hotel's high wall. She was obviously waiting for us.

Now it is perhaps hard for us to understand that she had been asked by the hotel staff to wait *outside*, and was actively discouraged from waiting inside, even though they knew she was waiting to meet us.

We had previously paid for her to stay some days with us at the hotel, and had realised then that this provoked a certain amount of bad feeling towards her from her own country people.

We were overjoyed to see her again. She looked absolutely beautiful in her bright, married-woman's clothing. We galloped down the street towards her, meaning to give her welcoming hugs. She saw us coming and squealed as only Kalyani can, and began to run towards us, but suddenly stopped, and stood quietly looking down at the ground.

We arrived in front of our Little Ant like a pair of noisy school kids, and I grabbed her and gave her a hug. Although she responded with a big grin, something was lacking. She smiled at Tod but didn't offer him a hug, and didn't even reach out to pull his beard. He sensed her reserve, and simply said how good it was to see her again.

I felt for him. I felt his disappointment.

In 2009 Tod and Kalyani had been great mates, and many a

time as I plodded flat-footedly along a mountain track behind the pair of them, puffing and panting, sweating, unable to keep up, I'd heard them laughing together, and Kalyani squealing and giggling as Tod told her stories about life in the UK. Listening to them used to make *me* laugh too.

But now she was a married woman, and her cultural background meant that she was expected to act accordingly. She was no longer the wide-eyed, carefree youngster who wanted to know everything we could tell her about the world outside Nepal, and who, like us, saw something funny in just about every situation.

We walked together into the hotel's small, walled garden, and ordered tea from the mildly disapproving waiter. We sat at a table amongst the huge pots of lush green vines and brightly coloured flowers that cast shadows here and there across the garden. They offered some respite from the relentless noon sun, and their aroma perfumed the hot air.

As we waited for tea to appear we began to show Kalyani some of the very many photos we had taken in 2009. We had been unable to send them to the village for fear they would be stolen in transit.

She was thrilled, and poured over them, laughing and giggling as she saw some of the funnier ones. The memories raced back.

She started to chat, telling us what had been going on in Salle recently. We heard about her sister's new baby, grandfather's bees, her father's possible retirement from teaching, the new village road…We loved it!

"These are for Woolly Dog," I told her when she paused for breath, pulling a couple of small, bone-shaped dog biscuits out of my pocket, "I've brought him 1kg, but he'll have to share them with his girlfriend!"

"Oh, Fiona!" Kalyani squealed, "Did I not tell you that Woolly Dog is married now, and he has a son!"

We all laughed.

Woolly Dog lived next door to the house that Tod and I had stayed in in the village of Salle. He was a gentle, bumbling giant of a canine, and we fell in love with him.

Dogs are not appreciated in Nepal, but of course in this cruel lack of appreciation the Nepalese are not alone throughout the world.

The Himalayan canines inhabit a sad, grey nether land, somewhere between the wild and the semi-domestic state – theirs is not a happy lot.

Their job is to protect the inhabitants of the house outside which they live, and this protection extends to the other village animals – goats, water buffalo, chickens and pigs.

I would just point out here that if you don't know that a mountain village has pigs, you are not likely to guess that fact. The pigs live their whole lives inside small wooden sheds, and never see the light of day.

"Well, I hope Woolly's glamorous girlfriend is the mother of his son!" I said to Kalyani, laughing.

"Of course, of course," she assured me, "she is faithful! They are married!"

I couldn't wait to see Woolly again. We had shared some adventures with him, and the last time we saw him we had left him tied to a desk in a small junior school in the village of Lohrimani, an hour's trek from Salle! The children took him home after school. It's a long story, and one which is told in detail in our first book.

We told Kalyani that we needed three days to properly acclimatise to the altitude before we attempted the trip back up to the village again. She understood.

Tea finished, photos looked through, and news caught up on, Kalyani stood up to leave. She grabbed Tod and gave him a bear hug! Then she pulled his beard! Our Little Ant was back again!

Chapter Four

Tod and I spent the next couple of days padding round our old haunts near the hotel. Every so often a shopkeeper would recognise him and come running out onto the street to hug him!

We were in and out of shops drinking Nepali tea until we could no longer face another cup of it.

It was March, and it was pretty hot, somewhere between 25 and 30C. We didn't venture outside Thamel, the tourist area of Kathmandu, and found plenty to do and see while strolling gently around the narrow streets of straw coloured, hard baked clay. The city we had known and loved two years ago was still alive and thriving, but we noticed some very obvious changes.

The first of those changes struck us immediately we set foot in the main shopping area of Thamel.

In 2009 it could at times be almost impossible to simply walk along the streets, let alone look at the wonderful array of goods on sale, because of the perpetual, and sometimes quite nasty harassment from the shopkeepers. They were all determined to sell you their goods, and in that respect were no different from shop keepers in many other parts of the world. However, more often than not they simply would not take 'no' for an answer, and frequently lost potential sales when the tourists got fed up being constantly pestered, and walked away, taking their currency with them.

But this time in Thamel we wondered if we'd become invisible!

No one accosted us as we wandered down the street. No one tried the 'hard sell' as we checked out the colourful displays of unusual, locally made clothing, and no one approached us as we played with the 'singing' bowls, or examined the attractive jewellery.

We were not even challenged when we **entered** a shop or

two...

It was distinctly odd, but was in fact a very welcome, pleasant change.

We assumed that the shopkeepers had formed themselves into some kind of association, and taken advice on the best way to behave around foreign tourists...

It was some time before we discovered that the advent of this unfamiliar behaviour amongst the Nepalese shopkeepers *wasn't* due to any new association, or any advice about curbing the hard sell, but was in fact due to the passing of a new law through the Nepalese Parliament. This law promised a substantial prison-term to any shopkeeper found guilty of harassing tourists.

It is, therefore, no wonder that we passed unhindered along the streets of Thamel that day.

The other immediately obvious change that struck us the moment we ventured out of the hotel was that the street dogs had all but disappeared from the whole area.

The streets had not been completely overrun with the dogs, but there had certainly been enough of them living wild there to give one pause for thought. They scavenged for meagre scraps of discarded food, living amongst the people, but completely ignored by them.

"Where are the dogs? What's happened to them?" I asked a pleasant young man who ran a tiny restaurant on the main street.

"The Kathmandu Council have moved them," he told me.

I wasn't at all sure what to make of 'moved them'. There is a total lack of regard for animal welfare generally in Nepal, and the organisation, effort and expense that would unquestionably be involved in any large-scale operation to shift the Kathmandu street dogs somewhere else, is something that even the RSPCA in the UK would doubtless baulk at.

I didn't like the sound of it.

A couple of days later I read in an English-language newspaper that the Kathmandu City Council had poisoned

10,000 street dogs in the Thamel area in the previous year.

The lack of electricity in Kathmandu is an all-pervading, ongoing problem to which there is, it seems, no imminent solution.

The majority of businesses have had to invest in generators or batteries to create their own electricity, although most cannot afford to run them permanently. Across the city the noise of struggling generators is an almost constant background roar by day, and throughout half of the night.

Lists of 'blackout times' – when the electricity is turned off – are published weekly.

We had to go to the Bus Station to get our tickets for the journey up to the village the day before we wanted to travel. Kalyani said she would accompany us there, and make sure we got the correct tickets at the right price. And of course she was coming with us to the village.

But on the Saturday she didn't show up at the hotel. We tried to reach her on her mobile, but because she lives in the Kathmandu suburbs her phone number is not a Kathmandu city number, so we had to use an international phone to contact her.

But there was no electricity at all on Saturday, so the international phones didn't work. Ergo, we couldn't contact Kalyani to see why she hadn't turned up.

It was another day before she arrived beaming and giggling at the hotel, and hugged us both. We didn't mention that she was a day late, and nor did she.

We all piled noisily into a taxi and set off for the Bus Station. The roads of the capital city had not changed much in our two-year absence, and we bumped and crashed, skidded and swerved, neatly avoided handcarts, cows, bikes, stray bricks and pedestrians, and twenty minutes later stopped with a jarring screech outside the massive metal gates of the Kathmandu Bus Station.

Dust swirled in small, twisting tornadoes across the pathway into the Station, encouraged by a brisk, warm wind. We covered our faces as best we could against the unpleasantness of grime in our eyes and mouths, and began to follow Kalyani as she expertly pushed and swerved her way through the throng of humanity milling around the huge gates.

Tod and I were both pleasantly surprised to see how much the place had changed for the better. In 2009 it had resembled nothing less than an open-air cesspit, with decaying rubbish, and human excrement spread everywhere.

Now the rubbish had at least been swept into a massive pile in the centre of the Station, making walking across to the ticket office marginally more agreeable.

The mind-boggling noise of the huge buses' engines remained as we remembered it, and the ear-splitting roar of several engines combined prevented any semblance of conversation, as we dodged between the massive metal monsters, trying to keep Kalyani in our sights.

We both noticed that one or two of the buses looked slightly newer than the rest, their tyres less bald. This was a very welcome step in the right direction, as Nepal languishes near the top of the international road-fatalities chart, and is not known for enforcing too many checks on the road worthiness of its public transport.

However, the world's greatest unanswered question remained: 'How the hell does *anyone* ever know *which* bus goes *where, from* where, and at *what time?'*

There was still a total lack of understandable signage or infor-mation in the Bus Station, which only added to the apparent chaos. The buses do not park in designated bays – there *are* no designated bays – and when parked they do not even all face the same direction.

A huge crowd of buses milled around, seemingly aimlessly, stopping here and there for a moment or two, picking up a passenger here, dropping one off there...

Suddenly there was a shout, barely audible over the ongoing scrummage. A man had lost his balance and fallen from the roof of a bus. We turned just in time to see him slither down the side of the metal monster, clutching at whatever he could to slow his descent. He was certainly not a young man – the tell-tale grey hair was exposed as his traditional Nepali hat slid from his head and landed some few feet from the bus.

The man hit the ground, shoeless feet first, and fell forward, but as Tod and I started to move in his direction to see if we could help, he stood up and brushed the dust from his clothing. Someone handed him his hat, and he brushed that off too. Then, unaided and uncomplaining he walked slowly to the bus's external ladder, and climbed stiffly and carefully up to the roof.

He sat back down beside the two goats that were travelling with him on the roof of the bus, seemingly none the worse for his tumble.

Tod and I looked at each other. Not for the first time we shared the overwhelming feeling that we wanted to do *something, anything,* to try to make life a little easier, a little less harsh maybe, for at least a few people in this amazing country.

Kalyani had reached the ticket office, tucked away in the far corner of the Bus Station, and was talking loudly to the clerk through the half-open window between them. Loud talking is a must during any kind of negotiation. We stood and waited. We knew by now that all transactions take some time in Nepal, and nothing gets done in a hurry.

The habitual crowd of Nepalese men hanging around the ticket office stared curiously at us. We smiled back.

Five minutes later Kalyani reappeared next to us.

"There are only two seats left on the micro bus tomorrow," she shouted, the only way to be heard above the ongoing commotion.

Our hearts sank. That meant yet another day's delay, and we were anxious now to get going.

"Ok. Book us in for the next day then please," we said.

The small, ten-seater micro bus has a marginally better road safety record than any other bus in Nepal. The large 'Local Bus' is notorious, with an appalling safety record, and to make matters worse, drivers have often been found to have drunk raxi before getting behind the wheel. Although efforts are being made to improve safety on public transport, it seems there is still a long way to go.

A few moments later Kalyani trotted back to us again and said,

"There are places on the Local Express bus tomorrow."

"No," Tod said, shaking his head, "Our rucksacks would have to go on the roof, so it's no."

The Local Express bus cuts about one hour off the usual eight, nine, or even ten-hour trip to the village. The roof is usually crammed with people and animals travelling on the cheapest tickets – actually, come to think of it, I don't know if goats pay at all – but the luggage *also* goes on the roof.

Sad to say it is often reported that pieces of luggage, especially travellers' luggage, do not arrive at their destinations intact. So there would be little chance of our two bulging rucksacks getting there without being rifled, and probably removed from the roof completely.

Kalyani nodded. She understood.

The ticket-office clerk shouted something in our direction, and Kalyani laughed,

"He says, 'Why not buy a seat for your rucksacks?'" she translated.

We looked at each other.

"Brilliant idea, Little Ant. That's what we'll do!" we said, grinning.

The ticket-office clerk was bobbing up and down, beside himself with pride for having had such a good idea!

"He's really pleased," Kalyani said, giggling again. "It's

maybe a while since he had such a good idea!" and we all fell about laughing. This was more like our wicked Kalyani!

And so the tickets were bought, and we were finally ready to go.

We had caused quite a ripple of interest around the Bus Station, and a small crowd had gathered to see what we were up to. There was great amusement over the seat we had bought for our rucksacks, and as we left the Station *we and our rucksacks* were loudly wished a happy journey.

Chapter Five

The hotel was full that night. Although we tried we couldn't get a room for Kalyani. So we smuggled her up to our room after dinner, and she had the spare bed.

We got up at 4am in the absolute blackness of a city without lighting, and bumbled about in the unfamiliar room, falling over each other and giggling and shushing one another (*how* old are we?) with only one small candle and a torch to light us. We collected the last of our stuff together and stumbled as quietly as we could down the stairs into the large, cool hotel lobby.

There, a couple of wavering candles sent the shadows racing unsteadily across the marble floor, and faintly illuminated the sleeping forms of half a dozen people sprawled out on various chairs and sofas. One of them was the night porter. He smiled sleepily at us, padded barefoot across the lobby, and kept watch at the hotel door for our taxi. All was quiet, save for the muffled harmony of gentle snoring around the lobby.

When our transport arrived Tod and Kalyani grabbed the heavy rucksacks and chucked them onto the taxi roof. I felt faint – they weighed 23kg each.

Tod and I scrambled into the back seat and wedged there like a couple of tinned sardines. Kalyani settled into the front. Within minutes she was asleep – she too, like Tod, could sleep on a clothes line!

Now you'd think that the streets of Kathmandu would be reasonably quiet at 5am, wouldn't you? You'd be wrong.

There are few street lights away from the city centre, and those that do exist of course had no power, so the streets were inky dark as we set off for the Bus Station.

At least in the daylight you have some hope of avoiding the potholes, piles of rubbish, cows, stray bricks and stones that are an integral part of the Kathmandu road system, but in the dark, well...

We went with the flow, and were thrown around in the small taxi which was driven, Kalyani told us, by a very careful driver.

Very careful driver or not, he couldn't avoid the obstacles sprinkled across the roads, and in fact he didn't seem to try. I wondered what the life span of a small Kathmandu taxi was, and as we leapfrogged across a particularly large pothole, I wondered anxiously if our rucksacks were still travelling with us.

Emerging from the narrow streets onto the wider roads of the more central area of Kathmandu, we hit a traffic jam.

We love Kathmandu traffic jams because they are unique in the field of traffic jams, and as long as you are not in a hurry, they are *fun*!

Our very careful driver slowly negotiated a path around herds of bicycles and motor bikes, all ringing bells or hooting at each other; a wooden box full of chickens, which had fallen from the back of something or other – its owner was trying to retrieve it – and an assortment of mostly grossly overloaded small vans which, interestingly enough, all seemed to be pointing in different directions.

Shoals of people on foot, most of them so loaded with goods that you could only see their legs, whipped backwards and forwards in front of the car. Our driver stopped to let a huge, misshapen cardboard box on legs pass in front of us, but instead the legs clambered over the bonnet, and with barely a pause trotted off. Tod and I laughed. Our driver didn't. He carried on, unfazed. Fazing rarely occurs in Nepal.

The Bus Station, when we arrived there, was almost as busy as it is at midday, and certainly just as noisy.

"I'll go and find our bus," Kalyani shouted to us, and vanished into the swirling melee.

Tod and the taxi driver had unloaded our rucksacks by the time she returned, and then we all set off to make our way through the massed ranks of assorted people, animals and goods, to our bus.

It was still only half light, so we couldn't really see what kind of condition the Express Bus was in when we reached it, but it looked as though all the wheels were on, so we climbed on board, taking our rucksacks with us.

Half a dozen weary Nepalese travellers were already on board as we found our seats. They called polite greetings to us, and smiled and shook their heads in wonder when we dumped our two large rucksacks together in a window seat.

A couple of minutes later Kalyani was nose to nose with the second-in-command of the bus. What do you know! He didn't want to accept that our rucksacks had their own seat ticket, and angrily told her to move them onto the roof.

Now, I would back Kalyani to win in an argument with just about anyone, and it took her roughly three minutes to see off this latest challenge. The ticket collector stalked off muttering loudly, glaring at us as he passed. We guessed he probably wasn't saying,

"What a nice lady you are. How glad I am to have met you."

Kalyani, completely unconcerned, was already settling down to sleep in the seat behind us.

We made ourselves as comfortable as possible in the restricted space.

"I'd forgotten how small these seats are," I mumbled. Travelling on a Local Bus always reminds us Westerners just how small the Nepalese people are, compared to us.

"Oh look, Tod!" I said, "There are handles on the backs of the seats in front...I wonder why."

No answer.

I stared at the thin metal handles, two on each seat back. Huuummm.

"I was just thinking," I said, "How can this Express Bus cut an hour off the usual journey?"

No answer.

"I mean," I went on, "there's only *one* route, and no shortcuts..."

Still no response. I turned my head and stared at Tod. He has rather a good repertoire of 'looks', most of which seem to be reserved for me alone. Not sure why. This one was a clever combination of withering and pitying, but before I could respond to it the bus engine sprang into life, and we were off.

I sighed, and turned my attention to the world outside the window.

We joined a noisy, slow-moving queue of buses, all jostling for position at the Bus Station exit. The congestion grew, aided and abetted by the fact that the exit was also the entrance. Tempers began to fray, and bus drivers and ticket collectors began to shout and gesticulate at each other.

The ticket collectors on each bus also double as the 'hang out the bus door and check how close we are to the sheer drop' person. They do a lot of banging on the side of the bus – one bang for *'OK, you can move forward'*, and two bangs for *'STOP!! WE ARE DANGEROUSLY CLOSE TO THE EDGE OF THE MOUNTAIN AND MAY DROP OFF AT ANY MOMENT!'* This kind of information is always very useful.

Our bus reached the front of the queue and paused at the roadside. The street sellers took this opportunity, and began hammering on the bus windows, trying to sell us water and fruit, falling over each other in their desperate haste.

Suddenly, with a roar from its engine, the bus catapulted itself out into the fast-moving stream of traffic like a camel on speed. We were rocked and thrown around, and there wasn't a person on that bus, driver included, whose bum remained in touch with the seat.

With a flash of inspiration I suddenly realised what the handles on the seat were for, and grabbed both of them. I managed to regain some kind of control over my movements, and thereby a modicum of dignity. I rubbed at my forehead, which had made contact with the top of the seat in front.

"Owwh!" I whinged, and glanced sideways at Tod. But he was staring out the bus window, fascinated by the mixture of sights passing by.

We careered down the main road out of Kathmandu, and I felt it prudent to retain hold of at least one seat handle.

"It won't be like this for the whole journey, will it?" I said to Tod.

"How do you think they cut an hour off the trip?" he answered, rather smugly, I thought.

I sighed again. We knew the route pretty well, having travelled it many times, but never at such a frenetic pace. We galloped along the flat floor of the Kathmandu valley, between the barely glimpsed steep mountains on either side, through the rolling clouds of grime, past the tall chimneys of the brick making factories, past the increasingly green patches of land, and finally *up*, as we climbed out of the valley.

The roads became tracks, clutching at the ever-steeper mountain sides, disintegrating into rubble and treacherous mud where the torrential monsoon rains had undermined them, causing them to collapse.

Gradually the air became clearer, cleaner, and the views became spectacular. We were climbing towards the top of the world.

"I see they still haven't invented the safety barrier," I said, as we looked down on a thin ribbon of blue river far below. There was only air between it and us.

We did indeed cut an hour off the usual journey, and arrived at Cowah ('The Village of the Damned' as we had named it, because of its uncanny similarity to the settings of many Hammer House of Horror films) around mid-afternoon.

The village of Cowah is situated in the Everest Region of Nepal, at the very top of a valley, about three hours trek from

Salle. Although small – it is no more than a collection of thirty or so dwellings – it is a sinister, dismal and dark place, and the people of Cowah seem dismal and dark too. They are nothing like as friendly as the people of Salle.

The best thing about Cowah is the chickens that live there. They are the Olympic sprinters of the chicken world, with a couple of long-jump finalists thrown in for good measure. We loved watching them.

As we rolled into the village the thunder crashed overhead and the rain began to fall in slow, heavy drops, turning the narrow road to mud in no time at all. High up in the Himalayas as we were, this weather is not uncommon, but I suddenly realised that I'd left our waterproofs in the hotel. Oh joy.

We stumbled out of the bus onto the side of the road clutching bags and rucksacks, and plonked down on the ground together in a tired heap.

The bus door creaked and groaned and slammed shut as it roared off, leaving a trail of fumes and dust hanging in equal portions above the road behind it.

Suddenly we heard a chorus of, "Namaste! Namaste!" from the other side of the road, and a group of people came running across to us, waving and shouting, their bright clothes contrasting starkly with the drab dullness all around.

Half a dozen villagers from Salle had come to meet us!

We were absolutely thrilled to see them again. We knew them all: Kalyani's father; one of her uncles (Kalyani holds the world record for having the greatest number of aunts and uncles), the village milkman, the bamboo-mat maker, and two women, mothers of children we had taught.

It was a truly emotional reunion – hugs all round.

They had made garlands from local flowers – a beautiful tradition of welcome or farewell – and draped them round us. It suddenly felt as if we'd never been away.

Apparently there were more villagers waiting to greet us at

Lohrimani, the next village down the valley, and one which we'd have to walk through on our way to Salle.

But first we had to have tea! So we all piled into a local house, and water was boiled on the open fire in the middle of the room. The villagers made us feel really welcome, and Kalyani and her father translated everyone's questions and greetings. There was a lot of laughter.

And then we all set off along the track out of Cowah towards Salle. The villagers wouldn't let us carry anything – just as well really, because I knew beyond a shadow of a doubt that I couldn't even *lift* my rucksack, let alone carry it down a mountain. What an unfit wimp I was. However, I was mortified to see that Molly, one of the children's mothers, had hoisted my 23kg bag onto her back, and just smiled and shook her head when I tried to remonstrate with her.

We were exceptionally fond of Molly. Let me tell you something of her life:

Six months before Tod and I first arrived in the village of Salle in 2009, Molly's husband, knowing that he had a serious illness, walked into the forest that surrounds Salle, and hanged himself.

This may sound unbelievably dreadful to our Western ears, but there is a certain logic in such a drastic course of action. There is *no* medication in the village, no doctors visit, no dentists call, and the nearest hospital is back up the valley to Cowah, and then twelve kilometres along the road to Jiri.

But medical treatment has to be paid for, hospitalisation is not free…In this remote part of the globe actually getting to the hospital is only part of the battle, a battle which may anyway be lost for lack of money.

Molly and her two children were living with her in-laws when we came to the village, and we passed the house every day on our trek to and from the school.

The house, like all the village houses, is made of local stone. It stands alone on a flat area of hard baked clay, with terraces below and forest around and above.

Molly's father in law, the gentle, softly spoken bamboo mat-maker, plies his trade at the front of the house, and you have to step over or around the half-finished weaves laid across the path.

You would need to search half the world to find kinder, genuinely nicer people than Molly and her in-laws.

Tod was fascinated by the bamboo weaving, so we used to stop every morning to watch. Molly would always ask us in for tea, so while Kalyani and I sat on the floor by the fire chatting with Molly, Tod would do a bit of weaving! He was pretty good at it.

We were invited to eat with the family on several occasions too – a great honour, as traditionally the village people do not eat in front of strangers. That was how we discovered that Molly makes the best raxi in the village! It seems she adds a secret ingredient during the distilling process...all very hush hush.

Now, raxi would take the top of your head off, given half a

chance, and could undoubtedly do a great job of cleaning the silver cutlery, or any old coins you might have. But you probably wouldn't want more than a mouthful of it at any one time. So when Molly took to offering us cups of raxi on our way to school, we had to politely decline!

Well, ok, there *was* one occasion...That was the day that the family's water buffalo, her burly calf, and myself, became entangled at a very narrow part of the track past the house...You really don't want to step between a hormonal water buffalo and her baby. Apologising just isn't enough.

Life in Salle does not revolve around the pursuit of money, but rather is still a case of growing your food, and exchanging what you have for what you don't have.

However, the need for money *has* begun to creep into the equation, as the traditional way of life begins, inevitably, to change. At the very least, the children's schooling has to be paid for – the uniform, books, paper and pens – and businesses in Kathmandu, and from abroad, will often, though not always, sponsor groups of children or whole villages.

In order to support her children through school Molly walks with a friend along the valley to a village roughly ten miles away, where they can buy bananas, mangos, and other fruit in season.

They collect what they can, and then retrace their steps past Salle, and continue on up the valley, and then up the mountain to Cowah. From there they walk the twelve kilometres along the narrow mountain road to Jiri.

Molly and her friend leave Salle in the early evening, and walk all night, usually reaching Jiri as the dawn breaks. They do this twice a week.

In Jiri they try to sell their fruit on the street, come rain or shine.

Jiri was the original Base Camp for Everest in the days of Edmund Hillary and Mallory. It no longer is, but it is still a thriving, though *very* small town by European standards.

Many climbers start their trek up to today's Base Camp from Jiri, and stay overnight in the town. So there is usually something of a market for Molly's bananas and other fruit. If luck is with her she may walk back to Salle with the equivalent of £2 in her pocket.

When we left Nepal in 2009 we took a ten-seat micro bus from Jiri to Kathmandu. The small bus terminal is at one end of the single street through the town, and Tod, Kalyani and I walked along there in the early morning light, as the shop keepers and street sellers began to set up for the day's trade.

It had rained heavily in the night, and the smooth clay surface of the narrow road was slippy. Tod kept a watchful eye on me, knowing my tendency to stumble over my own feet and catapult off into space at a moment's notice.

Jiri is high enough to be touched by the clouds, and we walked through patches of mist that left shining drops of moisture on our hair, and on Tod's beard.

Our bus was late leaving, and eventually pulled out of the terminal into a veritable scrum of mixed traffic, which leapfrogged erratically along the main street, ultimately moving only at the speed of the slowest vehicle.

Every so often our dubious progress was halted completely, and the driver banged his hands on the steering wheel in irritation, and spat a few words out – probably,

"Beautiful morning, isn't it? I *do* love this journey."

Tod and I watched, lost in our own homeward-bound thoughts.

Suddenly Kalyani shouted something to the driver, stood up and yanked one of the small, top windows open – the only windows in the bus that *did* open.

A group of street sellers were running alongside the bus, hoping it would stop again and we would maybe buy something from them. They held their goods up to the windows, desperate to tempt us.

But there, in the pushing shoving group outside, Kalyani had spotted Molly. She shouted to the driver to stop, but he ignored her. She *yelled* at him and he slowed down, just enough for Molly to push forward through the throng and shove a large bunch of bananas through the window. Molly shouted something to Kalyani, and then reached up and passed something else through the window. The driver put his foot down and we pulled away, but we heard Molly shouting after us,

"Tod! Fiona! Bye bye! Bye bye!"

We waved to her through the bus's back window, both of us awash with emotion.

Molly stood at the side of the road and waved until the bus rounded a bend, and we could no longer see her.

I sat back down in my seat and cried.

Kalyani handed us the bananas, and I cried some more.

"Please don't cry, Fiona," Kalyani said, "Molly took this from round her neck just now…She wants you to wear it."

And Kalyani handed me Molly's pretty red necklace, a traditional married woman's necklace, which she always wore.

Tod put his arm round me and gave me a hug, while I blubbered.

We were humbled by the unconditional generosity of a woman who had little or nothing in the way of material possessions, but would share what she had with us anyway, asking nothing in return.

Chapter Six

The rain stopped and the sun came out as we set off in a happy, noisy group along the track out of Cowah towards Salle.

Kalyani told us that the villagers had managed to collect enough money together to hire a bulldozer for a day, in order to dig a track from where we now stood, right along to a point just above Salle. We were looking forward to seeing it. *I* was looking forward to walking along it, as opposed to stumbling down the mountain side in ungainly, unladylike fashion, as I usually did.

But we were totally unprepared for what met our gaze within three minutes of leaving Cowah behind.

The new track had been gouged roughly and unevenly out of the mountain, and the heavy red clay that had been displaced by the bulldozer's work lay in discarded piles along the sides of the track, or spilled in thick, red rivulets down the mountainside and into the valley below.

The track cut deeply through what should have been a thickly forested area, but all that now remained of the once green and varied vegetation was a shocking, blitzed landscape of tree stumps, looking for all the world like a scene from the bombardments of the 1st World War.

The forest had been annihilated from a vast swathe of the mountain, leaving nothing to retain the topsoil during the heavy monsoon rains.

We were stunned.

There was even a new sawmill standing amongst all the devastation. Huge piles of tree trunks were strewn untidily around outside its doors, awaiting their further destruction. We stared as we walked slowly past.

"Are you replanting any trees?" we asked carefully.

"No," they told us.

The consensus was that those trees which had been felled

would soon grow again, without human help or intervention.

We made no comment, and felt it prudent to ask no more questions.

The forests of Nepal are considered to be more valuable today as timber, than as living trees...

We began to walk along the new track, our feet sinking into the soft clay. Tod and I gazed around at the sad remnants of the forest we remembered. It was very quiet.

And then there were stones on the track, laid there to prevent heavy trucks from sinking and sticking in the clay. They were large stones, unevenly placed, and unevenly cut. We began to laugh, all of us hopping from one stone to the next, Kalyani shrieking and giggling.

Thunder rolled around the valley and echoed off the mountain sides. Thick clouds began to boil through the valley below us. We looked down on them. How odd, to be higher than the clouds!

We had covered maybe a mile before the rain started again. Somehow it didn't seem to matter that we would surely get soaked. It wasn't cold or windy, and I was just so glad that we were *walking* to Salle, rather than scrambling there!

We suddenly heard an odd noise from the track behind us. It was a sort of grating, jangling, screeching roar, growing swiftly louder. We all stopped and stood listening, as the rain gathered strength.

Suddenly Kalyani yelled,

"Tod! Fiona! We've got a ride!" and she turned and positioned herself in the middle of the track just as a massive, brightly painted Indian-style truck rolled unsteadily round the corner, and lumbered noisily towards us. Gaily coloured ribbons and decorations hung, danced and jangled from every available point, as the truck rocked and swayed over the uneven, stone strewn surface.

Kalyani had more confidence than *I* did that the driver would see her and stop! But stop he did, within a few feet of our Little Ant. She was completely dwarfed by the enormous truck, and had never looked more like a munchkin. Kalyani ran to the driver's window and had a short, shouted conversation with him.

Tod and I exchanged grins. This was déjà vu 2009!

"In we get!" Kalyani shouted happily, beckoning to us, and she and the villagers began to scramble up the sides of the truck, into its open back. Our rucksacks were thrown in as if they were matchsticks.

I groaned. How do they do it, these people? They make it look so easy. *And*, no matter how difficult the journey, they smile.

Tod and I trotted back down the track to join our friends.

"Oh no," I thought anxiously as we neared the truck, "here we go again! How do I get up *there*?"

The massive tyres were taller than me. I felt an undignified flounder coming on.

The cab passenger door was suddenly flung open, and the driver leant across and shouted (shouting happens quite a bit in Nepal, I find),

"Here! Here! You two guests come talk with me! Come in here in my cab!"

I groaned again. I wasn't surprised to see that the helpful foot rest, for use when entering said cab, was set at a convenient height somewhere above my head.

"Come on, Fiona!" Kalyani yelled. I looked up. She was leaning over the side of the truck, grinning down at us, "You just jump up and we'll go!"

Oh yeah sure. I'll just jump up...not a problem.

I considered the merits of a whinge, but decided against it. I'd still have to get up there somehow. I sighed.

"You'll have to shove me up," I told Tod, "and no sarky comments please!"

Tod must have been tired I think, because it took two attempts before I managed to scramble, in my usual undignified fashion, into the cab.

This cab was smaller than the one in 2009. It was supposed to seat the driver and two passengers. I say 'supposed to' because there were already four people in there, so we of course made the total six.

I realised with a bit of a start that what I'd thought was the driver's multi-coloured coat, slung over the side of his seat, was in fact his wife. She was actually wedged in between him and the driver's door.

We got uncomfortably under way.

The noise of the huge engine, combined with the bumping and crashing as the truck staggered from one stone to another, and from one hole to another, was ear-splitting. Tod and I were jammed together, and rocked and swayed around in unison, every so often sliding forwards together into the windscreen, and pushing ourselves back onto the seat again.

The driver was a happy chap who couldn't believe his luck! He had a captive audience in his cab. His English was pretty good, and he wanted to chat about England, the USA, and the new Nepalese Parliament.

But we couldn't hear him above the ongoing racket, so he leant closer to us, somewhat alarmingly removing his eyes from the track and his hands from the steering wheel. Oh joy!

Now I don't know how often you've been squashed in a truck on a very bumpy track, high up in the Himalayas, but there must be few places less conducive to a friendly chat. We tried, but the lurching movement took our breath away, and we couldn't make ourselves heard.

We ended up laughing at the absurdity of it all! Every so often we heard Kalyani squealing, so we knew they were being thrown around too in the back of the truck.

Forty-five minutes later the driver stopped the engine and we all got out. The sudden quiet was *very* quiet. We had reached the point on the track nearest to Salle, and we would now have to trek down the steep mountain path and into the village. We were nearly there.

Chapter Seven

Tod set off down the steep track at a brisk trot – I really must have a word with him about watching too many Indiana Jones films. I limped stiffly after him, and Kalyani followed me, ready to catch me if necessary.

Suddenly the village came into view, and Tod and I stopped and stared across the gently sloping terraces below us, at the cluster of houses we remembered so well. The bright, early evening light accentuated the different colours of the crops on the terraces, and the many shades of green in the forest. The village had never looked so welcoming. It felt good, very good, to be back.

As we scrambled down the last bit of the path I saw a low, dark shadow disappear silently round the corner of the first village house.

"Is that Woolly?" I said to Tod.

"No," he said, "the fur was too dark. But it did look like

Woolly."

I put my hand in my pocket and checked out the dog-biscuit situation. Yes, I still had most of the kilo of bone shaped dog biccies that were destined for dear old Woolly's grateful gnashers. I couldn't wait to see him again.

We rounded the corner and were suddenly swamped by a noisy group of villagers who had been waiting for us to arrive. They descended on us in joyful chaos, and we saw all the familiar faces, and heard all the familiar greetings. It felt as if we'd never been away.

We were standing outside Kalyani's parents' house. It is the end house of a 'terrace' of three, and the view from the door is breathtaking. The house is over the hill from the one we stayed in in 2009, and looks down into a different valley, and far across the terraces towards the school.

Tod had disappeared under a veritable scrum of village women, all wanting to greet him. He emerged looking a bit rumpled – ah yes, the beard-pulling bit – but smiling broadly.

"Where's grandfather?" I asked Kalyani.

"Oh! He was in Lohrimani waiting for us!" she said, laughing, "The truck didn't stop there! Grandfather waved to us as we drove past. He'll be here soon. He's walking back."

Lohrimani is a small village, in fact the only village, between Cowah and Salle. Disturbingly, the vast majority of its inhabitants are related to Kalyani.

Looking around I suddenly realised that very few of the village women had come to say hello to me, and one or two even seemed to be giving me odd looks. They appeared unusually shy with me for some reason.

"Kalyani?" I said, "Is there something wrong? Have I done something to offend the women? They seem very quiet with me."

"Noooooo Fiona!" she said, laughing and grabbing my hand affectionately, "I've just told them who you are!"

I stared blankly at her.

"What do you mean?" I asked, "Why did you have to tell them who I am? They *know* who I am, don't they?"

"Well, Fiona..." and she started laughing again. The women had gathered around us and *they* started laughing too. They obviously knew something that *I* didn't. I looked at them in amazement. I hadn't realised they all had such short memories. I mean, how many white women had spent a number of months bumbling around in their village!

"Come on, Kalyani! Tell me!" I said, resisting the urge to laugh myself.

"You see," she said, still grinning, "when a Nepali lady grows older, she *looks* older. You know...she has lines on her face..." and Kalyani touched her grandmother's face – the unfortunate lady was standing beside me – just in case I wasn't aware what a wrinkle was.

"Kalyani!" I said, "I *know* what happens when we get older, but I *don't* know why you're telling me this."

"It is because you look younger *now* than you did two years ago! The women doubt who you are!" and, having translated this to the waiting women, Kalyani led the group in a rousing round of communal merriment.

Right-oh.

When it had died down enough for her to hear me I said, "So, you mean that because my hair is longer, and I'm wearing make-up, they think I'm a younger woman?"

"Ummm, yes, Fiona," Kalyani nodded, "and they think Tod is now with a different woman!" She fell about laughing again.

Well, ok...I admit that two years previously I had my hair very short. The women were always asking if it was short because it didn't grow for some reason. Huummm. *And,* I didn't wear any make up – our sojourn in the village had seemed a good excuse for a break from the old face paint. Ditto the nail varnish...

"Just wonderful!" I thought, "I make a bit of an effort, and look what happens! They think Tod's traded me in for a younger version!"

Finally the women came nearer and greeted me. They looked closely at my hair, and some of them ran their hands through it to see how it felt. They grabbed my hands and examined my nail varnish, oohing and aahing at the length of my nails, which weren't all that long, just longer than theirs, and not quite so broken. Aahhha, the tell-tale softy office-worker's nails.

There was a lot of giggling and pointing, particularly at my lipstick. I felt like a prize exhibit of the vegetable kind. But eventually all the inspection was done, and I felt welcome again in Salle.

So you see, it is obviously nothing short of miraculous what a bit of slap and some nail varnish can do for you, high up in the Everest region of the Himalayas, that amazing land within reach of the clouds.

Kalyani's mum took our hands and firmly propelled Tod and me into her house. The water was already boiling on the open fire in the middle of the floor.

Everyone who could squeeze into the small room sat down on the bamboo mats that were spread around the hard clay floor. There was a sudden hush as I anxiously contemplated the portion of matting awaiting my bum, and creakily lowered myself down onto it. Neither Tod nor I could manage to sit cross-legged on the floor – actually, I couldn't sit cross-legged anywhere at all...

A communal sigh of relief ran round the assembled group when I finally got myself settled, legs stretched out in front of me. I don't think anyone noticed my clenched teeth.

We all had Nepali tea, and heard more news from the village. Then Tod brought out the huge pile of photos we'd taken on our last visit, and began to hand them out. There was such excitement! Most of the villagers had never seen a photo of themselves, and you could have heard the squealing and laughter as far away as Tibet!

The shadows lengthened, and those villagers who'd been working on the terraces came back to the village. More hugs, more greetings, and more laughter. Kalyani's grandfather arrived, having missed us at the village of Lohrimani.

He is one of the village elders, and a kinder, more compassionate man you may never meet. He commands respect wherever he goes. He is very fond of Tod, and I have some great photos of the two of them wandering along a mountain track, grandfather's arm round Tod's shoulders, looking for all the world like father and son deep in conversation.

He was once, many years ago, involved in politics, and we were fascinated to learn that he rode a white horse in those days. There are no horses now in the Everest region of Nepal.

Tod spent that evening huddled with one group of villagers or another, looking through the photos. I sat with Kalyani, her sister and her mother, chatting and watching the fun.

Soon the flames from the fire became the only source of light in the house as night crept nearer, and Tod and I started to yawn.

We politely declined all offers of raxi, and decided to call it a day.

I needed a bit of help to stagger upright – my legs seemed to have fixed themselves into an unnatural position for a human, and they refused all 'walk normally' commands. I limped over to the door.

We said goodnight to everyone and walked a couple of steps to the side of the house, where the beam from our small torch picked out the rough wooden ladder leaning against, but not attached to, the upstairs wooden balcony.

With Tod holding the ladder steady I wobbled my way to the top and clambered onto the balcony. There was only one room up there, and it was Kalyani's. We went in.

There was a carpet on the floor! Wow! The only one in the village, and probably the only one this side of Jiri! We were impressed. How on earth had they got it up there!

There was also a wooden cabinet-type piece of furniture in the room, with Kalyani's books in it, and a couple of chairs. Some kind soul had brought our rucksacks upstairs, and someone had put a bottle of raxi just inside the door.

Best of all, there was a bed. I limped over and sat heavily down on it.

"Oh no!" I moaned, "How could I forget that they don't do mattresses!"

But we were tired. It had been a long and emotional day. We blew out the candles, slid gingerly onto the unwelcoming wooden slats, and tried to sleep.

Chapter Eight

We lay in the dark and listened to the familiar sounds of the village settling down for the night. Eventually that unique silence, a silence you find only amongst the high mountains of the world, enveloped us.

But we couldn't sleep. The bed was just too uncomfortable for our pampered Western bones, and we eventually got up and put the heavy, lumpy, eiderdown thingy between us and the hard wooden slats.

We were marginally more comfortable like that, though somewhat chillier.

Some time later I started to regret drinking that last cup of Nepali tea. How stupid was I? This wasn't going to be a quick trot across a carpeted landing into a warm, comfortable bathroom, with illumination at the flick of a switch...

Oh *no!*...I *had* to go. I knew it. I couldn't put it off any longer.

"Tod?" I tried, quietly.

No answer.

"Tod!" slightly louder.

No answer.

"Tod!" and I prodded a finger in the dark at where I thought his back, or maybe front, would be.

"Owwh! What! What?" he mumbled, still half asleep.

"Are you awake?" I asked. (How completely ridiculous was that question? They come out automatically, don't they?)

"No!" Tod mumbled. (So do those responses).

"I need to go," I told him.

"Ok," he said, and turned over, his back towards me.

"Well...so...I'll just go then?" I said, hoping I'd hit that magic, slightly whingy note, the one that usually gets results.

"Ok," Tod said, his voice muffled through the eiderdown thing.

"I'll be five or ten minutes probably," I told his back.

Silence. My whingy note may need some fine tuning.

I sighed, got up, and started stumbling about in the inky darkness, trying to locate my backpack and find the torch. I was acutely aware that I had no shoes on – it felt somehow odd to be walking on carpet here in the village – and I prayed that I was alone in the room, as I really didn't fancy standing on a spider or a cockroach going about their legitimate business in the dark.

I found the torch, and with its help located some clothes. I flapped them around a bit, hoping anything insecty would be dislodged. Then I sat on the edge of the bed and shook my boots. Nothing scurried out, so I put them on. I felt the need to hurry a bit, but I was dreading the next part of the expedition. A bit of moral support wouldn't go amiss.

"Tod?" I said.

Silence.

"Tod!" Louder.

"Yes? What?" he said.

There may well have been just a slight note of peevishness there.

"I'm going now," I said, walking towards the door.

"Ok."

"See you in a bit," I said, glancing back over my shoulder towards the lump in the bed. Then I unlocked the wooden shutters and stepped through onto the balcony, and into velvet darkness.

The night was spectacular, and eerily silent. There were so many stars in the sky that it looked strangely unfamiliar, like nothing I had seen before. A feeling of being totally alone in a vast, awesome emptiness descended on me – a mere mortal, glimpsing just the very edge of a corner of infinity.

I crept along the wooden balcony, sticking close to the wall of the house. There was of course no safety rail, and I felt a bit of a wobble coming on as I made my way by the light of the small torch, to the top of the ladder. I fumbled clumsily onto it, all hands and feet, grabbing at the top rung to steady myself. The ladder moved, grating against the balcony floor, protesting at my weight on it. I froze, and stopped breathing.

It seemed to settle, to adjust its position, but then sank to one side, scraping alarmingly, wood against wood. I squealed as I swayed atop the ladder. The ridiculousness of the situation wasn't lost on me. This was no place to break a leg.

By the time I reached the ground I was shaking, but at least I was down. I'd worry about the return journey later.

I turned and set off along the track, stepping through the small torch beam, trying to avoid the larger stones, and walking away from the comfort of the small cluster of houses.

The narrow path runs along the bottom of a particularly high and steep grassy hill on one side, and a 10ft sheer drop on the other. I knew the path, but I don't balance well at the best of times, and even in daylight, with the benefit of my glasses on my nose, I'm prone to wobbling about quite a bit on it.

I began to feel nervous. The darkness outside the beam of the torch seemed to move, to creep furtively towards me. I was suddenly sure I wasn't alone.

I tried to walk faster, but only succeeded in stumbling and stubbing my toe, sending mini avalanches of stones and grit over the edge of the path. They spattered noisily onto the bamboo roof of a pig hut below. My anxiety grew.

By the time the small toilet shed hove into view, clearly silhouetted against the star bright sky, I was breathing heavily and the hairs on the back of my neck were creeping. I grabbed at the door latch and tried to pull the old wooden door open. It resisted, and I suddenly remembered that Kalyani had told us it is padlocked at night now. *No!*

I fumbled around looking for the key, and eventually found it under a stone – just where Kalyani had said it would be.

The padlock undid easily, and I jerked the door open, stepped quickly inside and slammed it shut behind me. My heart was pounding.

What was *that?* I was sure I could hear something outside the door, a sort of odd breathing sound, separated from me only by a decaying wooden door.

The toilet shed was made of local stone and, like most of them in this part of Nepal, was roughly 3ft by 4ft, with a hole in the middle of the hard clay floor. If you are taller than 5ft you will have to stoop, and many a Westerner has given themselves a nasty cut on the head by standing up too far and too fast.

You are rarely alone in the loo; many nosey eyes often accompany your every move. I swung the torch beam quickly around, looking for snakes or spiders.

But peeping toms or not, I had to go!

All done, I turned to face the door. I don't like the dark, and I was more than nervous. What on earth was I *doing* bumbling about in the remote Himalayas in the middle of the night? My mum always said I had some strange ideas.

This time there was no mistaking the sound of breathing outside the door. And wasn't that the soft sound of feet…or *paws*, moving on the path, making a sort of gentle crunching sound on the loose gravel?

We had discovered in 2009 that wild tigers still visit the village, and on two occasions then a tiger had been scared away from outside the house we were staying in.

"Ok!" I thought shakily, "I'll open the door and scream for Tod."

That seemed like a really good plan, actually the *only* plan, so I slowly and carefully pushed open the old door, wincing each time it creaked, and stepped cautiously outside.

The torch beam lit the first couple of feet of the path. I braced myself.

Suddenly a black shadow, long and low, leapt in front of me! A dog's face, tongue lolling out between perfect white teeth, was caught in the beam, its eyes reflecting the light like bright gemstones.

"Woolly!" I said, "Hello *you!* How're you doing?"

But the instant I said it I knew this wasn't Woolly.

The dog ran round me, tail wagging frantically, panting and making little yelping noises. He was obviously pleased to see me. But this wasn't Woolly.

However, the similarities were striking, and even in the dark I could see that this must be one of Woolly's pups.

What a marvel of a thing is the canine instinct. This young dog had never met us, we had not seen him at all, except for the briefest of glimpses on our arrival in the village, and yet he somehow *knew* that I'd be as pleased to meet him, as he seemed to be to meet me.

For an absolute certainty he would not have dared approach any of the villagers in the same way. If he had, sad to say he would probably have been beaten or stoned for his trouble.

I started back along the path while my new companion dashed joyfully up and down the steep hill, his progress marked by little yelps and mumbles. He stopped in front of me every so often to say hello, panting and wagging, waiting until I touched him on the head, and then rushing away again along the path and up the hill.

He raced off into the dark at one point, and either through sheer exuberance or just not looking where he was going in the dark, ran straight into a tree stump.

There was a sharp yelp of a different tone, and a jumbled crash, as he rolled down the hill towards me. I could hear his progress, but couldn't fix the torch beam on him. I held my breath. He reached the bottom of the hill in a heap, some way ahead of me along the path. I started to run towards him, anxious that he had hurt himself. But he simply picked himself up, shook himself, and carried on, thankfully none the worse for his tumble.

Without a doubt this bumbling, loveable pup was one of

Woolly's lads. Like father, like son!

We arrived together, breathlessly, at the bottom of the ladder.

"You've probably woken the whole village!" Tod's voice floated down from the balcony. He was grinning. I should have known he wouldn't leave me on my own in the dark.

"What are you doing?" he asked.

"I've met one of Woolly's pups," I called up.

Tod came down the ladder in a much more sprightly fashion than I had.

"Well well!" he said, "Yes, I think you've found Son of Woolly! Or rather, he's found you."

We sat a few moments with the dog, and then went back up to our room. Tod found the dog biccies and threw a few down. Son of Woolly munched and enjoyed.

We told him to go on home. He wagged at us and sat down at the bottom of the ladder. He was still there first thing the next morning.

Chapter Nine

We had brought quite a hotchpotch of presents with us for the ten children who had been in our class in 2009. We had grown very fond of them, even though they could never find the courage to speak to us in English, despite all our efforts!

And those English children, and their parents, who had become 'pen pals' with some of the school children, following our first visit, had also sent a variety of items for them.

On top of that, several of our friends had given us money for the village.

Kalyani wanted us to go to the school the next morning, to meet all the children, and distribute the presents there.

"But we've only got sweets and balloons for the other kids," I told her, "so wouldn't that be unfair? We don't want to cause any problems."

We knew there were roughly eighty children in the school.

"Maybe we should just meet our class here?" I said to Kalyani, as she perched on the edge of the bed and rooted through my make up bag, "and avoid any trouble?"

"Nooo, nooo, Fiona," she said, drawing a thick line on the back of her hand with my lippy, "they all want to see Tod and you again."

At least, I *think* that's what she said – her voice was rather muffled as she applied my lipstick to her lips.

"Are you sure about this?" I asked uncertainly.

"Yes, yes, Fiona, quite sure. Where is your nail varnish?"

I handed it over and waited while she did a bit of nifty painting.

"Before we go to the school we want to go and see Woolly," I told her.

"Ok."

Five minutes later the three of us set off to climb over the steep hill at the back of Kalyani's house, and walk down to where we'd lodged in 2009. It only took us ten minutes. We arrived on the flat clay area outside the house and looked around.

Everything was just as we remembered it. The two other, smaller houses standing nearby looked just the same; the crops, corn and millet, planted at the side of the houses, were growing well; the view out over the valley, where the terraces dropped away sharply, seemed exactly the same...

But Woolly wasn't there.

In fact, no one was around, and an almost unnatural, heavy silence hung over everything. It reminded me of a film set when the actors had finished their scene and gone home. Nothing moved, not even the goats, standing silently in their shelter at the back of the terrace.

I was really disappointed.

"I wonder what he's up to," I said to Tod.

"Probably asleep and snoring in one of the water buffalo shelters," he smiled.

We climbed back up the hill to Kalyani's house, picked up our rucksacks full of presents, and followed the path out of the village.

Within five minutes we were walking through the quiet forest, and then out onto the track that runs along the very edge of the terraces, allowing us a spectacular view of the valley below, and the mountain range beyond. I tried not to look down – knowing how close I am to a drop seems to make my brain determined to throw me over the edge.

We were doing our Pied Piper bit again, collecting children along the way. They ran round us on the path, laughing and shouting. Yet again we began to feel we'd slipped in time, and never actually been away.

Sadly, the deeper into the forest we went, the more evidence we saw of indiscriminate tree felling. In parts it looked as though a massive scythe had run amok, tossing tree trunks hither and thither, like huge matchsticks.

Kalyani led us and the children in a rousing chorus of 'Old MacDonald had a farm', and we all fell about laughing when she insisted on repeating the 'woof woof' refrain again and again! The villagers working on the terraces laughed and clapped, and waved to us as we passed noisily along the track.

We heard "Namaste! Ali Baba!" and Tod smiled.

Kalyani told us that the teachers in the school were new to the area. She didn't know them. They had been brought in to replace her, *and* the other three teachers, who had also left the school in the last year or so.

The school hadn't changed. We stood at the edge of the forest, high up above the massive clearing, and took in the atmosphere. Not for the first time we marvelled at the view.

But the wooden school huts were locked, and there were no teachers in sight. The only children around were the ones who had come with us.

Odd.

Kalyani made a phone call, spoke for a couple of minutes, and then turned to us.

"I think it must be a school holiday day," she said. She looked annoyed.

Tod and I exchanged glances. Something was wrong. We knew she was fibbing because her nose grew several inches longer before our very eyes, but we thought it best to say nothing.

"Well, most of our class are here, so why don't we go back to the village and give them their presents?" Tod said.

Ahh, the magic words! The blue touch paper was lit, and we were smothered in squealing children.

Then they ran, laughing and shouting, trying to race Tod back up the hill to the forest. Kalyani ran with them, giggling as she went.

I trundled along behind the chaos, at a much more sedate pace.

Hey ho! Back to the village!

Once there, we emptied everything we'd brought onto the bed, and did some organising. Thirty minutes later we were ready for the fun, and for the next couple of hours we all laughed and cried in equal measures.

The children came in one by one, which was great because it meant we could chat to them, and make sure the thermal pullovers we'd brought for them actually fitted!

We gave each of them a bag with soap, toothbrush, toothpaste, socks, gloves, pens and shampoo. But of course they preferred the games, balloons, sweets, bubbles and make up! And who could blame them!

We'd brought some medication for a couple of children who had skin complaints, and some eye drops, plasters and antiseptic cream. Much as we wanted to leave pain killers, and other medication with the villagers, we knew that would be asking for trouble without Kalyani there to administer it.

We had put a small amount of money into envelopes for the children, and Tod handed one to each of them. We noticed that some of the children dropped the envelope, and some just held it in their hands, unsure what to do with it.

Eventually Kalyani said,

"They do not know what it is. You should open it for them and show them."

Sure enough, the children were not familiar with envelopes, and the small brown ones we handed out just seemed like a piece of paper to them. They didn't realise it could be opened, or that it contained something.

Without a doubt most, if not all of the children, had never before possessed any money.

We told them that it wasn't just Tod and me who had provided the goodies and money, but that friends of ours had also sent things for them. Kalyani told us later that the children were astonished that people who didn't know them, and who lived half a world away, wanted to give them something.

Friends of ours, Lisa and her daughter Kelsey, sent a bag stuffed full of pens, books, and games for their pen pal, a little boy called Lal. I handed him the bag and he simply stared at me, standing quietly, unmoving, in front of Kalyani's house. I opened it and showed him what was in it, and then showed him a photo of Lisa and Kelsey. When he finally understood that everything in the bag was for *him*, he cried silently, the tears rolling down his face and dampening his new fleece pullover.

Other friends, Sue and Ashley, had previously sent a parcel to the village destined for their pen pal, a lovely young girl called Parbatti. We worried that it would not arrive, as several letters and parcels from the UK had gone missing along the way, easy pickings for the unscrupulous, unfeeling opportunists.

But as soon as we saw Parbatti we knew she'd got the parcel – she was wearing the pink and white striped hoodie that Sue had sent, and it was her prized possession.

We gave what we could to the adults – mostly soap, toothpaste and shampoo to the women, and socks and vests to the men.

Now here's a curious thing – the socks, being new, arrived in pairs, as they do. But within an hour of distributing them, it seemed that every man in the village had *odd* socks, and some had only *one* sock. What on earth had happened? What had they done with them? Does Nepal possess a fiendish sock gnome?

As the day wore on the village seemed to be full of balloons – we'd taken three hundred of them – and of bubbles. The adults loved them as much as the children! It positively rained bubbles and balloons that day in Salle. And do you know what; we too rediscovered the fun of bubble-blowing!

Tod and one of the village men he was particularly fond of disgraced themselves. We all know the 'rude' sounds that can be made by running your hands over a balloon? If not, give it a go somewhere private.

Well, the two of them just loved it. Their rude sound making expertise knew no bounds, and the more noises they made, the more everyone laughed. When they started doing the appropriate accompanying actions, arm in arm, parading up and down in front of Kalyani's house, the children in particular screamed with laughter.

And the *sound* of laughter, from both children and adults is, I must tell you, the sound we will always remember from that delightful day in the village.

Chapter Ten

We had a steady stream of visitors that evening, and we remembered them all from our last visit.

Our room began to fill up with gifts which, despite our protests, the villagers brought to us: bottles of raxi, cups of buffalo milk, cooked potatoes, buffalo cream. Ah, yes, when you get a chance, try some buffalo cream! What a taste! Fresh, light, creamy, tendency to make you feel sickly if you overindulge...

Grandfather came to show us that the special 'bee handling' gloves Tod had brought for him fitted well, and the new reading glasses were a great help to him for close work.

Grandma was already wearing the thermal vest. We were pleased about that – she is very traditional, and we had wondered if she would refuse to wear it. But recently she had been feeling the cold...

Molly arrived with raxi for Tod and a pashmina for me. I started to try to hand it back to her, for it was surely one of her possessions, but Kalyani stopped me. It would be rude to refuse it, she told me.

Later, we sat with Kalyani and discussed the day's events. We talked about the children, smiling at their reactions to the presents – the squabbles over the gloves with knitted, stand-up characters on the fingers; the slapped on, zombie-look eye shadow and lipstick – first attempts! And half a dozen children all squashing in a line on *one* skipping rope; the oohhs and aahhhs as the kids opened the new books, and unwrapped the pens and crayons...

The sun started to dip, and long shadows crept into the room. The sounds of merriment continued from outside, interspersed with muffled bangs and squeals, as balloons burst here and there.

We thought we'd just about managed to see everyone, when a village lady stepped quietly through the doorway, and stood silently looking at us.

A small child in school uniform came in with her, and stood close to the woman's side, holding tightly onto her long traditional skirt. Neither of them spoke.

Tod, Kalyani and I greeted her politely, and I stepped over to the small pile of goods we still had, and began to put some soap, shampoo, socks and other things into a bag for the woman and her child.

The silence in the room suddenly struck me as odd. I looked across at Tod and Kalyani, both usually chatty and bubbly, and was slightly disconcerted to see them both standing quietly, looking first at our visitors, and then at me. I wondered what was up with them all.

But I didn't want the woman to feel unwelcome, so I walked across the room towards her and the child, smiling and holding the bag of goodies out in front of me.

The pair were standing just inside the doorway, in deep shadow. I wasn't sure if I'd met them before because I couldn't make out their faces, and I wasn't wearing my glasses anyway. What remained of the light of day entered the room around them, framing them, and making recognition even harder.

So it wasn't until I was just a foot or so away from them that I saw what the woman was holding.

A magnificent cockerel sat unmoving on her arm. Its legs were bound together with a piece of rope, the frayed ends dangling below its feet.

Call me naïve, but it just did not occur to me that there was anything out of the ordinary in this situation. It was a common occurrence to see villagers carrying chickens, or other livestock around. Nothing unusual in that.

I reached out and stroked the gleaming blue and turquoise feathers on his back. They felt very warm. He was indeed a handsome chap.

"Look Tod!" I said over my shoulder, "Isn't he lovely?"

Kalyani said, "Fiona…" and stopped.

"Yes?" I said, turning round to look at her. But she remained silent, and looked away.

Huuummmm.

I turned back to the little tableau in front of me, and smiled at the woman. She smiled back. The room was very still.

And then the woman raised one hand to her mouth, in that unmistakable universal gesture which means 'Eat'.

An awful silence descended on the scene. I stared, horrified, at the woman.

"You're joking!" I said, "No way!" and I took a step back, away from her.

"Oh no no no no no noooo Fiona! It is rude to refuse! Please do not!" Kalyani pleaded.

I turned and glared at her. Indignation slapped instant blinkers on me, and whispered in my ear that Kalyani was also in some way to blame for this outrage,

"We're *not* eating him! No way!" I said, probably much louder than I should have.

Suddenly, Kalyani stepped quickly in front of me, whipped the cockerel off the woman's arm with all the flourish of a professional magician, and dashed out of the room with it. We heard her going down the ladder much faster than I thought was prudent.

Silence returned to the room. No one spoke. No one moved.

A couple of minutes later Kalyani was back, minus the cockerel. She spoke a few words to the woman, and then turned to me.

"I've given him to my mother to look after," she said, "and I've told her," she indicated the waiting woman, "that we'll eat him later." She winked at me. She has no shame. I breathed a sigh of relief.

We all sat down on the floor to watch the little boy open his presents.

"You remember who she is, don't you?" Tod asked me, nodding towards the woman, "She lost her husband."

Yes, now I remembered. A matter of a few weeks before we arrived in the village in 2009 this woman's husband had hanged himself. Like Molly's husband, he too had been seriously ill. This quiet, dignified woman was left alone to bring up nine children.

We had given her money and some clothes, and had often wondered how she was getting on. So today she had brought us the family cockerel as a gift, to say thank you for what we had given her.

Could I really have handled the situation so badly, so insensitively? I felt ashamed.

After our visitors had left, Kalyani's mum called us downstairs to show us where she had put the cockerel.

He was settled in a small wooden hutch outside her house, safe for the time being from the unwanted attentions of the local cockerel bully boy.

Someone brought him some rice, and someone else brought him some water. The villagers were all really amused. They couldn't understand our concern for the welfare of animals, but nevertheless they respected our strange ways.

Tod named the cockerel 'Lucky'.

"You're not to eat him!" he told a group of giggling villagers, "We'll come back one day and there'll be trouble if he's in a pot!"

This incident, the 'Lucky' incident, added another string to Kalyani's bow. She now holds the world record for the fastest 'dash down a ladder with a cockerel'.

Chapter Eleven

The next morning we went once again to look for Woolly Dog. But as before, the area around the house was deserted.

"Even Miss Glamour isn't here," I said to Tod, referring to Woolly's dark-furred, attractive girlfriend.

"We'll come back later," Tod said, "Don't worry, we'll find him."

But I was beginning to think something was wrong. This was Woolly's house, and in all the months we had known him he had seldom ventured far from outside it.

We spent the day wandering round the village and terraces, talking to people, looking at the animals, and watching the children playing with some of the games we'd brought them.

One of the village children had asked us to bring her some badminton rackets. Don't ask me how he did it, but Tod managed to fit four rackets and twenty shuttlecocks into our bulging rucksacks. The little girl was overjoyed.

"Tod! You are wanted!" Kalyani called, as we sat outside the house in the sunshine, enjoying the view across the terraces. She trotted over and grabbed Tod's hand, pulling him back with her to the group of women she had been talking to. They had begun to harvest the millet crop.

Sitting together in a circle on the ground, the village women were using large, heavy, flat pieces of wood, rather like cricket bats, to hit the millet which was piled on the ground in front of them. This thwacking of the millet loosens the seed from the husk. It was then piled into bamboo baskets, which the women shook, throwing the millet seeds up into the air, and separating them from the husks.

They wanted Tod to have a go. The women knew he was game for anything. He'd ploughed a terrace with a water buffalo in the past, so *this* should be a doddle! Mind you, if I remember rightly, he *did* want to know where the brakes were when the buffalo got under way...and I *do* remember the buffalo giving him a really dirty look – they are masters of the dirty look, the buffalo.

I went and found the camcorder, and filmed the fun. I took loads of photos too – just as well really, because I forgot to press the 'record' button on the camcorder. Sigh.

Tod was a natural. You'd think he'd been millet thwacking all his life, and he received a standing ovation from the villagers for his efforts! Yippee!

Evening came, and we were invited to have raxi at the house we'd stayed in in 2009. The elderly couple wanted to see us. So we walked back over the hill, trailing maybe twenty assorted villagers and children behind us, and arrived once again on the flat area outside the house.

The couple were waiting there with their neighbours from the other two houses. I recognised Woolly's 'mum' and smiled a greeting to her. Woolly lived outside her house, and she would occasionally throw him leftover rice, and sometimes put water out for him. Little enough maybe, but still more than most Nepalese people will do for a dog, sadly.

Tod noticed that the little girl we'd given the badminton set to was crying, huddled in a group with her friends.

"What is it? What's the matter?" he asked, and her friends pushed her forward. She was trying to hide something behind her back. It was a broken badminton racket. A village boy had taken the racket from her, and used it to hit a tennis ball, hard. Ergo, broken strings. Good thing we'd brought four.

Tod sat down and started to try to repair it. The kids clustered round him, watching.

I noticed Kalyani was talking to Woolly's mum.

"Kalyani?" I said, "Would you ask her where Woolly is. We haven't seen him yet."

"Ok, Fiona," she said, and spoke to the woman for a minute or two. I waited. I think I knew then that something was wrong.

"She says he isn't here," Kalyani said quietly, "He hasn't been here for a week or two."

"Well, where *is* he?" I asked.

Kalyani spoke to the woman again, the woman responded, and then laughed.

Kalyani looked quickly across at me. I couldn't read her expression, but this was not looking good.

"What's going on, Kalyani?" I asked, and the tone of my voice obviously translated, even if the actual words didn't, because a hush fell on the group of villagers standing around us. Everyone was listening now. No one was smiling. Some of them glanced in my direction, but none could meet my eye.

Kalyani and the woman began talking again.

"Kalyani? What is it? What's happened to Woolly?" I asked after a moment, interrupting the conversation. But I didn't really want to know. I was afraid to know.

"A man came here, one week ago, Fiona. He took Woolly Dog

and his girlfriend away," Kalyani said, her voice low, her expression serious.

There was complete silence. No one moved. The clouds that had drifted down from the mountains across the valley brought a dank chill to the evening air. There would be rain soon. That seemed somehow appropriate to the moment.

"But...*why?*" I said, "Does she know who the man was? *Why* would he take Woolly away?" It didn't make any sense.

"She thinks the dog is still in the village," Kalyani said.

"If she thinks that, she *must* know where he is!" I said, glaring at the woman, "Ask her again Kalyani, *please*. She *must* know more than she's saying."

But the woman simply repeated that a man had come and taken the two dogs away. *She* appeared to find it amusing, although not one other person in the group looked anything other than dismayed.

I was devastated.

"Tod, Fiona, please don't be upset," Kalyani said quietly, "you are invited to take raxi," and she indicated the elderly couple who were waiting in their doorway. They looked concerned.

I didn't want to be rude, so I turned towards the door. The group of villagers and children filed quietly into the house and began to sit down on the floor mats.

But I couldn't go in. I couldn't smile. I couldn't laugh.

Tod stood up and handed the semi-repaired badminton racket back to the little girl. Then he came over and put his hands on my shoulders,

"We can't do anything, Fo. I know you're upset, but we can't do anything," he said gently.

"I know," I said, "but I can't pretend to be happy in front of everyone, so I'll go. I'll see you back at the room later."

I walked slowly back onto the path, and up the hill, away from the house, and away from the people who didn't care what had happened to Woolly. It must be many years since I'd sobbed like I did then.

I climbed the ladder, went into Kalyani's room and sat on the bed.

Ten minutes later Tod and Kalyani arrived back. They too had not been able to pretend to be happy.

Kalyani came and sat next to me on the bed. She took my hand, and wept.

It was only because I knew that *my* sadness was the cause of Kalyani's tears that I managed to pull myself together. I really didn't want to make her unhappy.

So I dried my eyes, passed a tissue to Kalyani, and Tod opened one of the many bottles of raxi that had materialised in the room during the day. We all had a swig.

"Tod, Fiona, I don't know what happened to Woolly Dog, but I promise I will try to find out," Kalyani told us as she left later.

I lay awake long into the night, and for once it wasn't the hard bed that stole sleep away from me. I didn't understand, none of us did, what had happened to Woolly and his girlfriend.

A dog barked in the deep silence of the night, the sound echoing along the valley and scaring a night hunting bird. It screeched into flight, and the dog barked again.

I sat up, the better to hear the bark.

"That's not him, Fo," Tod said quietly from beside me, "it's not Woolly."

Tod too was awake, listening and wondering.

The next morning found us both tired, but determined to smile and carry on as if all was well, for obvious reasons. It would be very unfair of us to dismay the normally cheery villagers.

This was to be our last day in the village anyway. Kalyani wanted to take us to visit her new husband's village, to see the house that was being built for them there. And she wanted us to meet her in-laws. How cool was that?

We'd be leaving Salle early the next morning, so we started to collect our things together, smiling as we realised that we had next to nothing now! I might even be able to carry my own rucksack.

That'd make a change!

Kalyani's father came into our room to see us. He is a gentle, refined man, headmaster of the small state school near the village.

His English is pretty good, so we chatted for a few minutes. As usual, we bemoaned the inescapable fact that our command of the Nepalese language did not extend further than 'Hello' and 'thank you'! He smiled kindly at us. Then he said,

"I am so sorry that the man Dhan has caused you such upset."

"Pardon?" I said. I didn't know what he meant.

"Dhan," he repeated, looking at us. Then, because we were staring blankly at him he said, "The school closed...And the dog...Woolly Dog..."

In a flash all became crystal clear. I suddenly *knew* what Kalyani's father was talking about.

"It was *him*? You mean *Dhan*?" I asked, leaning forward towards him, unable to keep the astonishment out of my voice.

"Yes," he said simply, quietly, nodding his head.

After Kalyani's father had left, Tod and I went to find Kalyani.

"Yes, I am so sorry, Tod and Fiona, and all the villagers are so sorry. These problems have been caused by Dhan," she told us.

Now that we knew, it made perfect sense.

Dhan had told the teachers to close the school; and had Dhan really been responsible for taking Woolly and his girlfriend out of the village? It is of course important to point out that we have no actual proof that Dhan had any involvement in the disappearance of the dogs, other than what the villagers told us.

But to explain all this to you, to explain *why*, I will have to take you back to the very beginning of our stay in Nepal in 2009, and tell you some things which were not mentioned in our first book.

Chapter Twelve

Before we went up to the village of Salle in 2009, Tod and I did a two-week trek through the Annapurna region of Nepal. I say 'Tod and I' but actually *Tod* was the one who did the trek, *I* did the ungainly and embarrassing slipping, tripping, puffing and sweating, with the odd, unladylike expletive thrown in here and there. I spent two weeks wondering if my swollen, painful feet would ever again trust me.

I should *never* have attempted to view the exquisite Annapurna region of Nepal from amongst its mountain peaks.

Few things in life are sure. But *this* is: I will never, ever, do that or anything like that, again! The very sound of the words 'trek' and 'Annapurna' still bring me out in a hot sweat!

We were a group of ten trekkers – no, make that *nine* trekkers and one complete plonker – with five or six Nepalese porters to carry our rucksacks and look after us. The head porter was a man named Dhan, and it was he who had asked for volunteers to teach English in his village – the village of Salle.

We met him in Kathmandu before the trek, and had of course no reason to think him anything other than welcoming. His spoken English was good, so communication wasn't a problem.

Dhan assured us that he would look after us, and sort out anything that we needed, and that included arranging any trips we wanted to do while we were in Nepal. That made life a lot easier for us, strangers as we were, in a country whose language we did not speak.

We told him that we wanted to spend a few days in the Chitwan National Park, a jungle area in the south of the country. We intended to stop there on our way back to Kathmandu, after the trek.

And then, we said, our great ambition was to visit Tibet, if the borders of that mysterious country were opened during our time in Nepal.

It was then March, and as it happened Tibet's border was closed to all foreigners until April that year, when it unexpectedly reopened.

Back in Kathmandu following the trek, and after a short stopover in the jungle in Chitwan, we found ourselves marooned for several days in the capital city by a series of public-transport strikes.

It was then that we began to notice one or two disquieting things about Dhan.

Whenever we went with Dhan in a taxi *we* would pay the fare. Ok. No problem. But *he* would always insist on handing the money to the driver, and he would never return any change to us. He did the same thing with the tickets on the micro bus up to the village, the first time we went there. The money he retained mounted up. We said nothing, but it niggled.

Stranded in Kathmandu as we were, we wandered around sightseeing, and called into several agencies which advertised trips. We were shocked to find that Dhan had charged us exactly double what it would have cost us to visit Chitwan, if we had used an agency ourselves, and cut him out as the middle man. *He* had simply paid an agency, and pocketed the difference. A simple way to obtain the equivalent of a couple of month's salary in Nepal.

We began to enquire at various places about a trip to Tibet. Dhan had already given us a quote for the trip, and was actually pressuring us to accept it. But we were delighted that we *hadn't* asked him to go ahead and make arrangements for us, because we discovered that he was going to charge us a *massive* amount, much more than any agency.

Then there was the mobile-phone fiasco. You cannot use a foreign mobile phone in Nepal. It won't work. So we needed to buy a Nepalese phone and sim card, which was, Dhan assured us, a simple task. He took us by taxi to a shop where we did indeed manage to buy a mobile phone. So, where do we get the sim card, we asked him.

"It is expensive, and difficult to find, but my friend will sell you a new sim card for half price," he told us.

"Great. When?" we asked.

"In a day or so," he said.

But in the interim, the hotel manager asked us why we hadn't yet sorted out a mobile phone. We told him that Dhan was getting us a sim card for half price.

"How much?" he asked us.

We told him. He raised his eyebrows.

"You are being cheated," he said, "Go to the shop over there, with your passports, and buy a sim card for the correct price." He pointed to a small general store round the corner from the hotel.

We did as the manager suggested, purchased a sim card, and saved ourselves the equivalent of £30 – a goodly amount of money in Nepal, and an amount which would simply have found its way into Dhan's pocket, yet again.

In the great scheme of things, none of these incidents is a huge deal.

However, they gave us a picture of the kind of man Dhan is, and we gained an insight into his way of thinking. We didn't like it, but we didn't say anything. We did not intend to let him distract us from our aim, and that was to teach English to the children in Salle.

Dhan lives in Kathmandu, but he appeared in the village two or three times during our stay in Salle. Some of the things he happily told us during these visits, about the way he makes his living, disgusted us. And some of the things we saw him do left us despairing of human nature.

We did not realise that anyone else knew about Dhan's attempts to charge us over the odds whenever he could – to rip us off – and we are still not clear how the villagers found out about it. But find out they did.

Towards the end of our stay in Salle, Kalyani told us that the villagers were angry with Dhan, and had told him so in no uncertain terms.

They couldn't understand why he would try to take money from us, when *we* were giving our time and energy to the school for free, and had brought books, pens, and a huge amount of other supplies with us for the school. We had also bought school books from both Kathmandu and Jiri, and lugged them back up to the village with us.

The villagers knew this. They appreciated it.

As a result, Dhan became persona non grata in the village, and that obviously rankled.

So, this unscrupulous man appeared unable to cope with the fact that Tod and I were going back to Salle eighteen months later. He was seemingly eaten up with jealousy at the thought that we would be welcomed back to the village, and had in fact remained in regular touch with Kalyani.

Dhan decided to try to spoil our return.

He phoned the school teachers, and told them to close the school and give the children the day off. As Dhan is on 'the board of governors' of the junior school, and was involved in the original establishment of the school, the teachers agreed, although they didn't know the real reason for the closure.

When it became known in the village that the school was shut on the day that Kalyani, Tod and I went there, the parents were angry. When they discovered that Dhan had ordered it to be closed, they were furious. Kalyani grinned as she told us that one village woman, who had access to a mobile phone, had rung Dhan and shouted at him,

"Who do you think you are? The Prime Minister of Salle?"

(It loses nothing in translation!)

As it turned out, it really didn't matter to us that the school was closed. The day was just about perfect anyway.

But what *did* matter, and what is eternally unforgivable, is the fact that *someone* removed Woolly and his girlfriend from the village.

We never found out what happened to Woolly and Miss Glamour. They have never reappeared in the village.

We do not know if the dogs were taken so far away that they could not find their way back, or if they were killed.

I still cannot bear to dwell on their fate, but it rests heavily on my shoulders.

For if we had not loved Woolly, this unconscionable act would not have befallen him, and that big, bumbling, affectionate comedian of a canine would have been there in Salle to greet us.

I believe that we pay a price, or receive a reward, for everything that we do in this life. Not one thought, not one action, no matter how small or seemingly inconsequential goes unnoticed in the final reckoning.

Eternal Law will *not* make an exception of whoever removed the dogs from the village.

Bless you Woolly, wherever you are.

Chapter Thirteen

We set off the next day to walk to Kalyani's 'new' village. Parbatti, one of the children from our 2009 class, came with us. Her house was along the way, and she wanted us to meet her mother again.

Leaving the village was the usual odd, emotional mixture of laughter and tears. We were smothered in flower garlands, and daubed with red tikka. We took a lot of photos, in which both Tod and I resemble outsize garden gnomes.

Grandfather said he was worried he'd have died before we came back to see him again, but we promised not to leave a return visit too long.

Molly said she'd walk some of the way with us, and half a dozen children said they would too.

We eventually took our leave, amidst a chorus of "Bye bye! Bye bye!", and climbed out of the village and onto the path towards Lohrimani.

Half an hour later we had reached that amazing point which is actually a mountain ridge. You are walking a path right along the pointy top of the mountain, with a deep valley either side. It is here that we would usually turn right, and take the path down into Lohrimani. But Kalyani called,

"Fiona, Tod! This way!"

She was pointing down into the valley on the other side of the mountain. She had often told us that the weather in that valley was unusual, as if it had its own micro climate, very mild in winter, and very hot in summer. The inhabitants were able to grow a large variety of vegetables and fruit, including melons and outdoor tomatoes, and different, more prolific crops from those grown in Salle.

"My new village is there," Kalyani told us, indicating a spot in mid air, as she lent out above the almost vertical rocky drop that tumbled down to the far away valley floor, "It is at the end of the river," she said smiling.

I could not see the river. We were so high above the valley floor that I could barely make *that* out, let alone anything meandering along it.

I drew back from the scary edge and looked around. The vegetation lining the track was green and beautiful, the day was bright and warm, my rucksack weighed next to nothing, and I was looking forward to ambling down into the valley in time for tea.

"Tod! Fiona! Come on!" Kalyani's voice drifted up to us from over the edge of the valley side, accompanied by the sound of pebbles and small stones sliding and bouncing downwards in determined avalanches.

"Where are you going?" I shouted, alarmed. I ran to the edge, looked over, and almost fainted as I saw Kalyani climbing, well *scrambling* actually, down the almost sheer mountain side, "What are you *doing*?" I shouted, my voice an octave higher than its comfort zone.

"I'm going to my village. Come on both of you!" she called up.

"Ahh, ummm, Kalyani," Tod said calmly, "Is there another way down? This path is maybe just a bit steep for Fo."

"Just a bit steep," I gasped, "*A bit steep*? Are you *mad*? This is the north face of the Eiger!"

Kalyani reappeared on the path, wearing her best quizzical expression.

"Oh, is it too steep for you?" she asked innocently.

I didn't doubt that Tod would be able to make it down to the valley floor, but probably not with me on his back, and that was the only way I could see *myself* getting down there.

"Ok. No problem, Fiona and Tod. We can walk round," Kalyani said sweetly, and I looked at her suspiciously.

"Walk round? Which way?" I asked.

"We can go to Lohrimani and take the track from there," she

said, "It's easy."

"How long will it take us to get to your village? Tod asked her.

"Oh, not long," Kalyani told him, and started to walk off down the path. The children scampered after her.

"Well, how long is 'not long'?" Tod tried again, grinning.

She stopped and looked round at us. It was one of those unforgettable moments that imprints on your memory, and is still there years later – our Little Ant, smiling prettily in the sunshine, framed against the silk blue sky, on top of a mountain, high in the remote Himalayas, her nose almost imperceptibly adding a centimetre or two to its length.

"Maybe two hours. Not longer." And still smiling, she trotted off down the path, beckoning us to follow her.

Now, one thing you don't want to do in Nepal is to ask a Nepalese a question starting with 'How long?' or 'How far?' And you certainly don't want to ask *any* question containing the words 'trek', 'easy', 'difficult' or 'steep'.

This is a vital piece of information I'm passing on to you here, because there are no words in the Nepalese dictionary that mean 'difficult', 'hard', 'steep' or 'easy'. These words are deftly replaced by the oft used phrase 'little bit up, little bit down' which, roughly translated, means 'probably difficult, probably high and steep, probably have to climb'.

Whopper telling is a Nepalese national pastime where distances, journey times and treks are concerned – they can't help it, they have all drunk from the same whopper-telling bottle.

"Did you happen to notice that her nose grew a bit longer?" I asked Tod, and we both laughed. We were well aware that 'two hours' was probably going to be a conservative estimate!

But, hey ho! No problem! We had all day.

Down the track we went, laughing and talking as usual, Tod and I gazing around at the incomparable scenery. Lohrimani came into view, and as usual we were ambushed there by Kalyani's relations!

Thirty minutes later we had finished Nepali tea, and off we went again.

This time the track we took was unfamiliar to Tod and me. It was new since our last visit, and had been roughly hewn out of the heavy red clay. The imprints of the tracks the bulldozer had made were still visible, and we had to walk carefully between the ridges it had left. The path twisted back towards the way we had come, all the time descending lower into the valley.

As we walked the scenery changed. It became drier and dustier, the trees thinned out and the habitual conifer gave way to smaller, less green varieties.

Eventually my legs began to point out that they shouldn't be taken for granted. We had been walking for nearly two hours! There were very few houses around, but Parbatti pointed to a small cluster in the distance up ahead, and told us that she lived there. That cheered my legs up, and they put on a bit of a spurt.

Parbatti does a three-hour round trip, six days a week, to get to school. She is never late, never complains, and never stays off. This is not unusual for the children of the Everest region.

As we neared Parbatti's house we noticed an elderly lady sitting outside another, neighbouring house. She sat cross-legged on the ground, shoulders drooping, looking down, her shawl pulled over her head – a picture of abject misery.

"Is she ill?" Tod asked.

"Her husband has just died," Parbatti told us.

We had nothing left to give her. All our soap, shampoo and clothes had gone.

"I'll give her this," Tod said, fishing some money out of his pocket. He started to walk over to the woman. She heard his footsteps, looked up and saw him coming. She stood shakily up, gathering her long shawl around her. She looked more than a bit afraid to see a tall, hairy foreigner striding towards her, but

Parbatti called over, reassuring her that Tod meant her no harm.

When the woman saw what Tod was holding out to her, she began wailing loudly. So, having handed the money over, Tod beat a hasty retreat. The woman sat heavily back on the ground again, tears streaming down her face onto the traditional clothing she wore.

"She says you don't know what your kindness means to her," Kalyani translated, "She has no animals, no food, and no family. She is desperately unhappy."

"What can we do for her?" we asked. To just walk away seemed so callous.

"Don't worry," Kalyani told us, "Parbatti's mother is looking after the woman. They are treating her as one of their family. She won't go hungry or cold."

Huuummm. I wonder if *my* neighbours would feed me and look after me, if I ever found myself destitute? We seem to have lost that true feeling of community, that willingness to care for others, asking nothing in return. Collateral damage, I suppose, in our rush to 'develop' here in the West.

We walked a little further and saw Parbatti's mother waiting for us. She asked us into her house and made Nepali tea. Several of her neighbours came in through the windows. You know, I'm not sure *why*. It wasn't as if the house didn't have a door.

Parbatti offered us buffalo cream. Working on the assumption that it would have been rude to refuse, I accepted. Yummy!

"Don't forget, it makes you feel sickly," Tod said.

I pretended not to hear him.

"We could make this at home," I said.

"How?" he asked.

"Well, look," I said, "all they do is put the milk in a cool corner of the room, and leave it there for twenty-four hours. Then, bingo! You've got your cream on top. How hard is that?" Goody! I had a new project.

"Where would you get the milk from?" Tod asked. He does

sometimes ask daft questions.

"From a buffalo, of course," I said...Aahhhh, yes. Bit of a problem there maybe. Not many water buffalos in the north of England at the moment.

Tod stared at me. This one was a crafty mixture of pity and amusement.

Right-oh. I deserved that.

We took photos, thanked Parbatti's mother very much for her hospitality, and hugged Parbatti. Then we walked back onto the track, and turned our steps towards Kalyani's new village. At the first bend in the track we stopped and looked back. Parbatti still stood where we had left her. She was crying.

The further we went, the more clearly defined the valley became. Its high, steep mountain sides closed in on us, and the flat valley floor became narrower and greener, especially along the banks of the small river that flowed softly through it.

The vegetation had undergone a gradual transformation, and now seemed greener and more jungley than elsewhere. The track wended its way over to one side of the valley, and ran along next to the sheer mountain side. We began to see signs of cultivation here and there, but no habitations. It was very quiet, and very still in the valley. Our voices echoed off the precipice above us, reminding us just how extraordinarily high it was.

We had walked for something like two hours since leaving Parbatti's home, and I felt justified in having a bit of a strategic whinge.

"I'm hot, and my feet are getting sore," I said, "How much further is it Kalyani?"

"Less than one hour," she said, grabbing my hand and pulling "Come on! Not far now!"

Oh yeah, sure. I'd heard that one before. Tell that to my feet.

Another hour later, and still walking, we found ourselves in what could best be described as a green and very pleasant land. But I was finding it hard to appreciate the scenery because my feet had swollen, making walking uncomfortable. And my eyes were suffering from the glare of the hot sun off the white surface of the track, even through my sunglasses.

I was wilting. I needed to sit down.

"But we are nearly there, Fiona," Kalyani said.

I carefully ignored her, and sat down on a convenient large boulder at the side of the track. It was really good to take the weight off my grumbling feet.

Tod joined me on the boulder. He appeared disgustingly fresh. We looked around.

We had reached a point where the valley narrowed considerably, to no more than a few hundred yards across. Up ahead we could see what looked to be the end of the valley, as the massive mountain walls appeared to almost touch across it. Kalyani's new village must be up in those mountains somewhere, I thought.

We were sitting in a scene taken from a classic painting. Trees lined the river banks, and the sunlight glinted in bright shards off the gently flowing water. We had not seen anything like this kind of landscape before in Nepal.

We had stopped at the edge of an area of cultivated land, and as we looked around we saw a man across the other side of the field, ploughing with a handy water buffalo. He noticed us, grinned and waved.

We waved back. He was the only person we had seen since leaving Parbatti's.

Kalyani joined us, and we all took a well-earned breather. It was very peaceful in the valley, the silence accentuated by a noticeable lack of birdsong. The higher the altitude, (we were at about 7,000 feet), the fewer birds are able to survive there, no matter how attractive the environment.

"Look!" Kalyani said, smiling. She was pointing towards the man on the field.

The water buffalo had spotted us, and stopped in its tracks. It was staring at us, unmoving. The man was trying to persuade it to move on. He was probably shouting "Giddy up!" or whatever you say to a stationary water buffalo. We smiled, and returned to our relaxation.

A few moments later Kalyani said,

"Look!" and we turned again. The water buffalo had ignored the man's orders, and was still staring at us, unmoving. Actually, I think it was glaring, rather than staring. There is a difference, especially with water buffalos.

The man had produced a thin bamboo stick and was thwacking the buffalo on its back. This paltry punishment had absolutely no effect at all; I doubt the buffalo felt even a slight twinge, and it certainly didn't get moving again. It had become a statue.

But I began to feel that the buffalo was staring at *me*. I do have an odd relationship with water buffalo, and I was starting to feel awkward. But I wanted to sit just a bit longer, to give my feet a chance to cool down and to get my breath back – never an easy thing to do at that altitude.

The peace in the valley was almost a living thing, and the air was so fresh and clean that it seemed new, only just created, never used.

Then Kalyani started to giggle. Once again we turned to see what was going on behind us.

The poor man had cast aside his stick and was now attempting to *pull* the water buffalo forwards. He had his arms around its neck, in a none-too-subtle headlock. The buffalo looked as if this kind of thing happened all the time – he had not budged an inch, and did not seem in any way fazed. (Fazing rarely occurs in Nepal). His inscrutable gaze remained firmly fixed on us. Well, on *me*, to be precise!

Time to go!

We stood up and set off again, suppressing the urge to giggle and look back at the ongoing struggle of wills that we had caused. We thought it prudent not to wave goodbye to the unfortunate man, but we wondered how long it would take the water buffalo to get back into gear.

Pretty soon the path began to climb steeply. It was a well-constructed path, neat and smooth, with a water channel running alongside. The water made a gentle gurgling sound as it sped past on its journey down the mountain. In the distance up ahead we could hear the sound of a waterfall, and on turning a corner, it came into view. Tod and I stopped and stared.

The water was tumbling over the top of the high precipice, bouncing off the rock wall on its way down, and collecting in a small, deep, clear pool at the bottom of the mountain. From there it was channelled into the irrigation water course that followed the path back down into the valley. Wow. Impressive.

We climbed higher and higher. I was puffing and panting, concentrating on the one-foot-in-front-of-the-other bit, wishing I hadn't eaten so much buffalo cream. I was determined not to tell Tod that.

We were following the path as it cut through the mountain. I started to wonder where it would come out, and where Kalyani's village was.

And then, suddenly we were there, standing at the entrance to another valley, staring down its glorious length.

Tod and I looked at each other. This was just astounding. A small valley, one of the most beautiful you could imagine, stretched away into the distance in front of us. For just one moment I felt we could have been in Kent, or the Lake District, so 'un Nepalese' was the view. It had been taken straight out of someone's green and fertile imagination.

The valley sides were steep, almost vertical, and the flat floor was chequered by a number of diverse crops, growing in patches of differing colours and heights. Kalyani pointed out tomatoes – which only vaguely resembled our Western tomatoes – wheat, barley and potatoes. There were other crops, too, that we did not recognise.

And there were animals here and there: my friends the laid back water buffalo; chickens scurrying busily here and there, and nosey goats.

"We've stumbled into Shangri-La," I said to Tod, "What a brilliant place!"

The path led us straight through the centre of the valley, past the small, neat fields, where just a few men and women were working, to its far end. Here the mountains formed a veritable curtain right across the valley floor, and sealed it into its own privacy.

This was where the only houses in the valley stood, clustered together at the end.

We were welcomed warmly by Kalyani's parents in law. Her father in law is a Sherpa, which is a distinct ethnic group originally from the high eastern Himalayas. Sherpas tend to be taller than most other Nepalese, and he was certainly at least six-feet tall.

This softly spoken, immensely strong man showed us round, and answered our questions about the wonderful, secluded valley he called home. He also talked about the treks he had done in the past, carrying supplies for mountaineers, and Kalyani assured us that her father-in-law had reached the summit of Everest on two occasions. We believed her.

Fifty or so people live in the valley. Many of them are new arrivals, and there is quite a bit of house building going on. There is no actual village as such, more a collection of dwellings, much like Salle.

The houses are truly lovely to look at, made of wood and whitewashed local stone. They blend well into the environment. As in the village of Salle, they are virtually empty inside. Not a western comfort in sight!

In each house there is one room downstairs, with an open fire in the middle of the floor. The fire provides light, and all the cooking is done on it.

There is no kitchen or bathroom, and there are no chairs, no cupboards, no sofas. Actually, there were not even the usual bamboo floor mats. You just park your posterior on the hard clay floor. There are no electrical appliances, and no radio or TV.

Kalyani proudly showed us the house which was being built for her and her husband. Even at that early stage of construction we could see that it would eventually be lovely. We took lots of photos, and noticed that the builders were fascinated by the camera. So we took photos of them too. That evening Tod and I sat on the ground outside Kalyani's in-laws' house, looking down the peaceful valley. The sun was setting, its last rays covering the whole tranquil scene with a pinkish pastel hue. The view could not have been more stunning.

Kalyani was cooking for the builders. They sat in a circle on the floor of her in-laws' house, a dozen of them, smoking, talking, laughing, and drinking raxi. The smell of rice and dhal drifted out around us. We had already eaten our hard-boiled eggs and chips – Kalyani was a dab hand at that meal now!

"I could live here," Tod said dreamily.

"Not *permanently*?" I asked anxiously. Should I start worrying? Should I start one of my lists? What about inoculations? Oh dear.

"Maybe," he said, staring off down the valley into the rapidly advancing dusk.

"You need a good night's sleep," I told him, "and anyway, you wouldn't be able to ride your trike here. There's no petrol, and the tracks are too small and rocky. It'd tip over. You'd never get it up here in the first place." I was aware that I was babbling nervously. Tod smiled.

"Come on!" I said, and we both stood up and climbed the stairs into 'our' bedroom, hopeful of a good night's sleep.

Chapter Fourteen

"What are **they**"? I asked Tod, as we closed the door behind us and looked around the room.

'They' were three very large cylindrical containers, each about five-feet tall, with a diameter of maybe six feet. They were made of wood, and stood together in the middle of the small room.

"They're full of grain," Tod said staring into the nearest one, "Must be the harvest".

"Huummmm. What sort of creatures are fond of grain?" I wondered aloud, "Apart from mice and rats – I'm ok with them…Ummm, do spiders like grain?"

I really hoped they didn't.

Aside from the grain containers and the bed, the small room was empty. The glassless window next to the bed was covered by a heavy wooden shutter which, when opened, revealed a spectacular view. The moon and stars now shed a ghostly silver haze over the valley, and threw thin black shadows everywhere. Wow.

The bed was up there amongst the highly commended in 'The Hardest and Most Uncomfortable Bed Ever Built' competition. We fiddled around trying to find something to take the edge off the cutting hardness of the wooden slats, and finally decided to put the lumpy eiderdown thingy over them. That of course left us chilly, so we didn't undress, and put our coats over us too.

It wasn't long before Tod was snoring. I lay uncomfortably and listened to the unfamiliar sounds of the valley settling down for the night. The builders noisily finished their raxi, and some of them left the house. The others simply curled up on the floor downstairs and slept where they were. Perhaps the raxi helped to make the hard floor somewhat softer for them.

In no time at all there was complete silence.

Some time later a very strange sound reached my half-asleep

ears. I had no idea what it was. It came again, a sort of whooshing and tapping noise, sounding very loud in the quiet darkness of the house.

"What's *that*?" I asked the still snoring Tod, "Hey, Tod, what's that?" I repeated, and shook a conveniently close shoulder none too gently.

"What?" he mumbled, "What's the matter?"

"What's that sound?" I said. "Listen!"

It came again, louder, this time accompanied by a sort of dragging, scratching noise too.

"Don't know what that is," Tod said, yawning, "Go back to sleep."

"You don't think it's a spider, do you?" I said. Now, I *was* aware as I asked that question that it was probably a particularly stupid one to ask. But then, you never know, do you?

The sound came again. It seemed to be coming from inside the house somewhere.

"What could it be?" I said, rather breathlessly.

Silence.

"Tod! What could it be?" I tried again, louder.

"Haven't a clue," he mumbled.

"Well, couldn't we find out?" I said, "I mean, we don't want to be murdered in our sleep, do we?"

Tod has occasionally been known to call me a nag. I'm sure he doesn't mean it though, and he didn't actually say one single word as he got up, found the torch, and opened the bedroom door.

I heard him walk softly to the top of the stairs, pause, and then come back into the room.

"That'll be a first," he said as he got back onto the bed.

"What?" I asked, "What did you see? What do you mean 'that'll be a first'?"

"It'll be the first time a couple of humans have been murdered in their bed by two cockerels," he said, pulling his coat over himself and settling down again, "Here!" he said, handing me the torch, "Go and have a look!"

I did. Teetering on the top stair, I peered down into the gloom of the small, unlit hallway below. The whooshing and tapping sound came again, making me jump.

But I could see what was causing it now!

There was a cockerel under a conical-shaped bamboo basket in the corner of the hall. These baskets, which have plenty of holes woven into them so the cockerel or hen can see out, are used to safely isolate a bird for any number of reasons.

But this chap had been discovered by another cockerel, who apparently couldn't believe his luck. Every so often he lunged determinedly at the basket and its unfortunate occupant, pecking and pushing at it. The captive, obviously aggrieved by the indignity of the whole situation, retaliated by charging at his attacker, dragging the basket with him. The basket had become a protection and a hindrance at one and the same time. Neither bird was able to lay a beak or claw on the other.

Two things struck me as odd about this late night skirmish. The first was that neither cockerel made a sound – there was no crowing, screeching, or avian name-calling. Could it conceivably be that they didn't want to wake the household?

And secondly, don't most birds tuck themselves up safely somewhere when darkness falls? I didn't think cockerels were night prowlers, but maybe this opportunity to have a peck at your rival was just too good to miss.

I went back to bed. Tod and I giggled about the silent tussle going on downstairs. How long would it last, we wondered?

Some time later I was again awakened by a noise, and this time Tod was awake too.

"What on earth's *that*?" I whispered. This time the sound was definitely coming from outside the house.

"Sounds a bit like an engine," Tod said, "but it can't be."

Every thirty seconds or so a deep, groaning-type noise would start softly, and build quickly to a crescendo. This loud noise continued for a couple of seconds, and would then judder gradually away into silence. Weird!

We looked out the window. Nothing that we could see moved in the now almost completely dark valley. The noise was coming from away over to our left, beside the mountain wall.

It went on and on, at regular intervals, echoing eerily across the valley.

"It must be some kind of animal," I said.

"Probably," Tod said, and yawned.

"Do you think it's in pain?" I asked him, but he was already asleep again.

I woke several more times during the night and heard the same odd, disturbing noise. I worried that it was an animal in distress, and I hoped someone would help it.

I have most certainly slept better on many occasions than I did that night. I awoke weary and stiff, and still anxious about the fate of whatever had made that weird noise.

Tod and I wandered outside into a bright, fresh day. Work had already begun on the fields, and the builders, seemingly none the worse for their raxi session, were measuring wood and marking out an area for another house. Chickens and goats were getting in everyone's way.

Kalyani brought us tea and a smile.

"What was that noise in the night?" I asked her.

She looked at me blankly.

"What kind of sound?" she asked.

I demonstrated. Tod laughed. Kalyani frowned.

"It came from over there," and I pointed across to the side of the valley. Kalyani looked in that direction, but shook her head.

"I don't know, Fiona. I will ask for you."

Tod was interested in what the builders were doing. They crowded round, showing him this and that, explaining how they did things without the benefit of electricity or machinery.

Kalyani reappeared. She was giggling. This is not always a good sign with her!

"Fiona!" she said, linking her arm through mine, "Look over there. What do you see?" and she pointed to where I had told her the strange sound came from in the night.

"Ummmm, I see the side of the valley," I told her.

"Look up a little more," she said, still giggling, "just a little bit more."

"Aahhhhh, well...," I shaded my eyes and peered, "there's a water buffalo in a shelter maybe fifty yards up, just before it gets really steep," I said.

"Yes! Yes!" Kalyani said, laughing and pulling at my arm. I always find her laughter infectious, so I started to giggle too.

"Do you mean it was the water buffalo making that noise?" I said dubiously.

"Yes, Fiona! Yes!" she said.

"But water buffalo don't make that kind of noise!" I said, lamely.

"They do when they snore!" Kalyani said, and fell about laughing.

"What!" I said, "No!"

"Yes! My father-in-law has built a shelter on the mountainside especially for that water buffalo because she snores very loud. So he built it away from the house and the other animals!"

Right-oh. Interesting explanation for the creepy noise in the night.

Those of us with partners who snore may wish to consider our options.

Shortly after, we collected our stuff together, said goodbye to everyone and took our leave. We walked back through the valley and beyond, to a point where, apparently, we could take a bus to Kathmandu.

Chapter Fifteen

We waited at a spot high up on the side of a mountain where, Kalyani's father-in-law assured us, the bus to Kathmandu would stop. The track was steep, rocky and isolated, perfectly in harmony with the landscape around us.

There was just one house in sight, and the lady who lived there came and spoke to us. She brought her tiny baby. We took photos.

I wondered where the bus was coming *from*. How many people actually lived in this part of Nepal? There was no obvious way of making a living up here, no suitable land to plant crops on. How strange to find ourselves in such a desolate spot, within an hour's walk of Kalyani's beautiful valley of Shangri-La.

The familiar creaking and grating sound of a bus coming down the mountain track reached our ears, and it arrived in front of us with a flourish of dust from its tyres and a squealing of brakes.

We said goodbye to Kalyani's father-in-law and climbed onto the bus, taking our empty rucksacks with us. There was no point putting them on the roof.

The bus seated twenty-five, and there were already five or six Nepalese travellers on board. We settled into seats near the front, Tod and I together and Kalyani behind us. Off we went at a surprisingly sedate pace, and we stared out the windows at the awesome Himalayas passing by outside.

The track ran round the side of a mountain, and the bus bumped and rolled along, occasionally screeching almost to a halt to avoid a landslide or boulder in its way, throwing us forward into the back of the seat in front.

We continued for about an hour and then stopped in sight of a cluster of houses. The landscape was slightly less inhospitable now, and there were several trees dotted around which, in the absence of any terraces, actually managed to grow out of the mountain side itself. They looked out of place there, rather like an odd, rogue hair on a woman's chin.

A group of people were waiting for the bus, and when the door opened they crowded noisily on board.

There were plenty of free seats, but this group seemed, inexplicably, to want to stay at the front of the bus, and the seats there were quickly taken. We watched in amazement as three people happily crammed themselves into the two seats in front of us.

When all the seats towards the front of the bus were full, instead of moving back down the bus to the empty seats behind, everyone remained standing in the aisle, jam-packed tightly together, like books in a bookcase that was far too small for them.

We were open-mouthed with wonder! How very strange. What on earth were they doing?

"Maybe they're not going very far, and want to be first off?" I suggested. But that didn't seem likely.

By this time the jumbled human crush was edging noisily back down the aisle, as the sheer force of numbers compelled it to expand. Tod was sitting in the window seat, and we had our empty rucksacks by our feet, so our already restricted space was even more limited.

Laughter and loud talking filled the bus. No one seemed at all put out by this unnecessary melee in the aisle. Someone passed a baby over several heads – even the baby didn't seem put out.

The noisy throng moved further down the centre of the bus, and eventually arrived on a level with us. A rather large lady, wearing a bright blue sari, took up position next to my seat. She looked down at me and smiled. I smiled back.

More people got on the bus, and amid much laughter the melee was again forced to expand back along the aisle. The large lady fought bravely to retain her position next to me. She was standing sideways on to my seat, her back to me, and she suddenly reached out a hand and grabbed one of the handles on the back of the seat in front of me. She hung on grimly as the noisy tide swept past her, squashing her backwards onto me. I moved over towards Tod as much as I could, which wasn't much at all, to give her some more space to expand into.

Her blue-clad posterior began to inch towards my knees, and as I looked on in horror, it edged onto my left knee and began to settle there.

"Hey!" Tod called to my new friend, "There's plenty of room at the back!"

His words were lost among the noisy jollity in the bus, so he reached out and tapped her on the shoulder,

"There are lots of seats at the back!" he tried again, mindful of the encroaching posterior.

But to no avail. The lady just glanced over her shoulder and smiled at us. It looked as though we would have to travel in this odd, unnecessarily cramped fashion until they all got off.

The bus got underway again.

We looked out the window and realised just how high we were, and how close to the edge of the track the bus was. We were looking down on the tops of trees, and way, way below us we could see a river winding through a ravine. It looked like something out of Toy Town from this distance.

The track began to descend the mountain, and the standing crowd stumbled and swayed, clutching at whatever they could to stay upright.

It made no sense to Tod and me that they were still standing at this point, given the number of empty seats in the bus.

The track became steeper, and the bus slowed to a crawl. I began to feel nervous – we were certainly very close to the edge. I'm sure I've mentioned before that the safety barrier has not really put in an appearance yet in Nepal.

Suddenly the bus stopped, and there was a moment of hush as the roar of the engine died away. Then the door opened and the standing passengers began to pile out. The blue-clad posterior was withdrawn from my knee, and the woman disappeared down the bus steps. Even those travellers who had been seated now stood up and exited the bus.

Tod said

"Look!" and pointed at the sun-baked ground outside the window. There were several people on the bus roof, and we could see their shadows clearly outlined on the ground by the strong sunshine, as they too stood up and climbed down to the ground.

I looked round. Apart from us, and Kalyani, we were now alone on the bus,

"So they were only going a short distance, that's why they didn't sit down," I said, "There must be a village or a market round here, and that's where they're all going."

Tod looked doubtful,

"How's Kalyani?" he asked.

I struggled to turn and peer through the space between the tops of our seats, to get a view of Kalyani in the seat behind.

"Ahhhhhh," I said, "She's asleep. She's got her coat over her head," and Tod and I looked at each other and smiled.

"Noooooooo, Fiona!!" Kalyani's voice, muffled through her coat, startled us.

"What?" I said, "What was that Kalyani?"

"I am not asleep, Fiona!" she said, "I am afraid! Very afraid! I do not want to see!"

"Why?" I asked, "What's the matter?"

But before I got an answer to my question the bus engine roared into life, and off we went in jerky fits and starts, down the increasingly steep track. I turned away from Kalyani, and braced my hands against the seat in front to stop myself slithering into it. Tod did the same.

The track descended the mountain in a series of hairpin bends which were far too tight for the bus to negotiate. So it had to stop and reverse, then pull forward again, three or four times at each turn.

I was absolutely horrified.

"How on earth will he be able to get round *this* corner?" I demanded, my voice several octaves higher than normal, as we saw what was up ahead.

"Don't worry," Tod told me calmly, grabbing my hand, "he must have done this journey a lot, so he'll know the track."

That really didn't reassure me! I heard a kind of low squealing noise coming from under the coat in the seat behind, and I presumed that Kalyani wasn't reassured either!

Picture it: A severely steep track, barely wide enough to accommodate the wheels of a local bus, descending the mountain by means of the tightest of tight hairpin bends, high in the remote Himalayas, with not a cat-in-hell's chance of any help should we slide or skid off and crash down the mountain. On board, two plonkers and a faithful friend.

My stomach lurched, my hands were clammy, and I was shaking. I could not bring myself to look out the window, unlike Tod, who appeared disgustingly cool about our latest jaunt.

"That's why they all got off!" I squeaked, *"They're* not stupid!"

Those twenty minutes of hair-raising, slithering, engine-screaming descent that it took to reach a plateau, where the track became almost flat, were the most frightening twenty minutes of my life. We had tackled high roads before, but nothing like this.

Then the bus stopped, and the door opened. Everyone who had got off at the top of the mountain now got back on the bus, having done the sensible thing and climbed down!

Kalyani emerged from under her coat, grinning sheepishly.

This time there was no question of an unseemly scrum at the front of the bus. Everyone found a seat, no one stood. Panic over.

"Have there ever been any accidents here?" Tod asked Kalyani.

Personally I'd rather not have known the answer, but Tod

does have a morbid streak.

"Ummmmm...Yes," she said, nodding, "But only two."

"How bad?" he asked. I glared at him.

Kalyani told us that both buses had slipped off the track, and plunged right down to the bottom of the mountain. There had been no survivors on either bus.

The rest of the journey back to Kathmandu went remarkably smoothly, I'm pleased to report. By the time we arrived there, some eight hours later, my heart had recaptured its usual rhythm, and my hands were no longer clammy.

We spent another couple of days in the capital city, wandering happily around sightseeing with Kalyani, and drinking tea and chatting with Karma.

Then we said our goodbyes, and promising to return again in the not too distant future, took our leave.

And so ended another memorable sojourn in Nepal, a beautiful, astonishing country, which has made us laugh and made us cry; a country which has shown us glimpses of the very best of human nature, and contrasted that with the very worst of human behaviour.

But most of all, Nepal has changed our lives.

We will always keep a special place in our hearts for the villagers and children of Salle, and of course for our own Little Ant.

Keep up to date with books by Fiona Roberts at:
www.spanglefish.com/fionaroberts

BOOKS

O is a symbol of the world, of oneness and unity. In different cultures it also means the "eye," symbolizing knowledge and insight. We aim to publish books that are accessible, constructive and that challenge accepted opinion, both that of academia and the "moral majority."

Our books are available in all good English language bookstores worldwide. If you don't see the book on the shelves ask the bookstore to order it for you, quoting the ISBN number and title. Alternatively you can order online (all major online retail sites carry our titles) or contact the distributor in the relevant country, listed on the copyright page.

See our website **www.o-books.net** for a full list of over 500 titles, growing by 100 a year.

And tune in to myspiritradio.com for our book review radio show, hosted by June-Elleni Laine, where you can listen to the authors discussing their books.

mySpiritRadio